"Some people talk *about* the Bible. Other people know the Bible and show you their photos *of* the Bible. Then, there are those rare few who get a van and take you on a road trip *through* the Bible. This is one of those books. Mikalatos hits the nail on the biblical head—simply breathtaking. Put on your seat belts, roll down the windows, and bring some snacks. The trip is worth it."

A. J. Swoboda, pastor, professor, and author of *A Glorious Dark*

"I imagine that, not too long ago, a heap of superb storytelling and a pile of gospel-infused passion collided, with a peacock tail of sparks, and the result was Matt Mikalatos's *Into the Fray*. This book achieves the heroic by making millennia-old Scriptures feel fresh and distilling spiritual wisdom without being heavy handed. Read this book and see Jesus again for the first time!"

Jonathan Merritt, author of *Jesus Is Better Than You Imagined* and senior columnist for Religion News Service

"Christian truth doesn't change, but the way we express it does. It falls to believers in every generation to retell the Jesus story for their context. That's precisely what Matt Mikalatos has done in *Into the Fray*. With stirring images and buoyant prose, he reimagines the book of Acts in a way that is both faithful and fresh. Mikalatos breathes new life into the ancient, holy stories you thought you knew."

Drew Dyck, managing editor of *Leadership Journal* and author of *Yawning at Tigers: You Can't Tame God, So Stop Trying*

"The good news of the gospel doesn't change, but the settings for its telling are never static. Matt Mikalatos seems to understand that better than just about anyone. As he demonstrates with *Into the Fray*, Matt is a master storyteller and Jesus sharer with an uncanny gift for casting Jesus in a contemporary light and demonstrating his enduring relevance for this (or any) time."

Tom Krattenmaker, *USA Today* contributing columnist and author of *The Evangelicals You Don't Know*

"The greatest spell an author can cast is to tell a story that everyone knows, but make them *hear* it for the first time. With *Into the Fray*, Matt reminds us that the earliest days of the Christian community were days much like ours—fiery and rough, full of friendships and hanging trees and impossible odds, full of the wild, the mundane, the sweet, the bitter. Full, in a word, of the things God does to make himself known to the whole world. *Into the Fray* is relentlessly imaginative, unquestionably interesting, full of fun and play and well-made prose. Matt has written a rare treasure for readers: a theological page turner with heart."

Paul J. Pastor, author of *The Face of the Deep: Living into the Life of the Spirit*

"Matt has a gift for making the cloudy clear, for giving life to stale words on the page, for pulling readers into the fray. He once again brings the first century to us, and we find in this book an exciting call to be transformed and a reminder that the world will change for the better as we are changed by the Spirit of a living God."

Clay Morgan, author of *Undead: Revived, Resuscitated, Reborn*

"Most churches today claim to emulate the early church, but they lack the bold, fearless vision of our first fathers and mothers. With *Into the Fray*, Matt Mikalatos challenges us to see the early church with fresh eyes, to discern how the Holy Spirit drove them far past the boundaries of good religion to a resurrected life that can only be called revolutionary. Matt provokes us to dream that the Spirit isn't done with us, that God is still making a way in this world and calling the church to follow."

JR. Forasteros, teaching pastor of Catalyst Community Church

Into the Fray

Other Books by Matt Mikalatos

My Imaginary Jesus
Night of the Living Dead Christian
The First Time We Saw Him

ADVENTURES OF VALIDUS SMITH

The Sword of Six Worlds
The Armies of the Crimson Hawk

Into the Fray

HOW JESUS'S FOLLOWERS TURN THE WORLD UPSIDE DOWN

MATT MIKALATOS

BakerBooks

a division of Baker Publishing Group
Grand Rapids, Michigan

© 2015 by Matt Mikalatos

Published by Baker Books
a division of Baker Publishing Group
P.O. Box 6287, Grand Rapids, MI 49516-6287
www.bakerbooks.com

Printed in the United States of America

Library of Congress Cataloging-in-Publication Data
Mikalatos, Matt.
    Into the fray : how Jesus's followers turn the world upside down / Matt Mikalatos.
        pages cm
    Includes bibliographical references.
    ISBN 978-0-8010-1631-8 (pbk.)
    1. Church and the world. 2. Christianity—Influence. I. Title.
BR115.W6M525 2015
232—dc23   2015005952

The Author is represented by Ambassador Literary Agency, Nashville, TN.

15 16 17 18 19 20 21   7 6 5 4 3 2 1

To Krista, who gladly said,
"Take me to the riots" in Mexico City
and has gone with me
into the fray all over the world.
Here's the book
you've been waiting for all these years.

God created humanity because he loves stories.

Jewish proverb

Contents

Contents

Salutation

Dear Theo,

The hardest part of telling this story is knowing where to start. You say, "Start at the beginning." But with a tale this huge, which beginning should I choose?

Do I start with the breath and presence of the Almighty One hovering over the face of the chaotic waters in the everlasting darkness? Do I describe the flicker of radiation that poured into a bursting flood of illumination at the first words of creation? That moment may not be *the* beginning, but it's certainly *our* beginning. That would be an interesting place to start, listening in as the great Teacher taught creation its own existence.

I could start with the royal line, tracing back the kings and queens and ruffians and scoundrels and thieves who brought us to the moment of the Teacher's coronation, establishing his credentials to sit upon the throne of Israel and, eventually, every nation. I could tell it like that, the hero's tale, the history of the King. I could recount his journey from poverty to riches, from obscurity to infamy, from life to death and life again. I could regale you with the descent from heaven and the ascent to the throne. This story could fill bookshelves.

Or I could begin by first telling you the trick of the story: here it is, the story about the good news of Joshua, Jesus, the Chosen One, the Son of God himself. You'd listen all right, thinking it was a straightforward telling, but then I would tell you ancient words from ancient mouths and show you how this story is nothing new at all, that it's a story that began before we were born and it's as if we woke up and found ourselves in the middle of it. The place we think is the beginning is really the climax, the triumphant rising action, and just when we think all is lost, we discover ourselves living in smaller stories, the denouement, the falling action, the resolution.

Many others have told the story in those ways. Like grandmothers with faded photographs, those who lived through those days turn the pages tenderly and say with deep affection, "The first time we saw him, we didn't know what to think. He pulled a dead girl from her hearse and danced with her. He spoke words that astounded the crowds, or filled them with anger, or wonder, or confusion. He spit in the eyes of the blind, and they cried in joy to wipe away the spittle, their first sight his kind brown eyes."

You've heard all those stories. You've been taught all those things. You know about God, the King, the Chosen One, the one who will save us, the Ever-Living One, the one who sits at God's right hand, the one who is both God's Son and God himself, the Teacher, our brother, our friend, Joshua, Y'shua, Yesu, Isa, Jesus.

How will I tell the story?

By telling you *their* stories, the stories of the people who walked with him, listened to him, followed him. I'm going to lay it out, orderly and in chronological order. I'm interviewing them all face-to-face, and I'm writing it out so you can read it once and for all, in one place, and know that everything you've been taught is true. You'll get the final draft in time, but here are my notes, or some of them at least.

I've written you before to tell you stories, starting with Zack and Liz and the messenger in the darkness of the church. Do you notice how often God's work starts in darkness? I told you of God's promise that those who have walked in darkness will see a great light. I told you about Miryam, just a girl, stumbling over the dirty clothes on her floor when an angel appeared and told her she would be pregnant with God's Son. The garbage collectors and mechanics who came to see him, wrapped in a blanket and sleeping with his mother on an inflatable bed in a converted garage. The decrepit old man who burst into prayer when first he saw Jesus. The wrinkled apple of a woman who thanked God for the baby. A hundred other stories—of fishermen and IRS agents and theologians and billionaires all knocked off balance and drawn into the orbit of this uncommon man.

You know their stories because their stories are ours, just as our stories are theirs. They are the tales and happenings and accounts and reports of the good news about Jesus and about his life and death and teachings and coronation and return.

That's how I will tell the story. How about you? Where does your story of the Teacher become our story of the good news? Where will you begin?

I look forward to hearing your story. I'll share the interviews and rough notes and stories I've collected—the stories of still more people who have crossed paths with our beloved Lord.

With affection,
Dr. Lucas

1

Beautiful Feet on Distant Mountains

Three days after the army left, the people of Troy wait, breathless, upon the city walls. A few soldiers remain with the women and children and old men. Everyone knows they are nothing more than an honor guard. If the enemy crests the hill coming from the west, these soldiers can do little else than fall on their swords, or wait and hope that help might come before those in the city eat each other, starve, or burn.

Alexandros was too young to go to war. He tried to slip into the ranks as they left, but he was too small to make a convincing show of pretending to be a man. His father turned him back before they passed through the city gate. He bent down, his wrinkled face already covered in dust from the feet of the Greek army, took Alexandros by the shoulders, and said, "My son, this battle is not for you."

"But, Father, the Persian army is so large. The elders say that every man will be needed."

His father turned his head, watching the grand army make its way through the gate. Crowds lined the road, shouting encouragement and cheering the soldiers. Many wept in the crowd, calling out their last reminders of love to those going to war. "It's true, Alexandros. The Persians are strong as bears. Not one city has stood up to them, Son, not in the last decade."

"All the more reason, Father. One more blade, one more shield on the line. Let me join you. Please."

His father sighed. "You don't know what you ask. The most likely end to that tale would be father and son together in Hades, with your mother and sisters weeping on the far shore. Unless the Persians send them to join us too, gods forbid."

Alexandros felt his whole body wilt like a sun-scorched plant. His face burned hot with shame. "Taso is going! I can't stay with the women and boil stew while my friends spill blood."

The tail of the soldiers' column had almost passed through the gate. Time was short. "Son, you have a job the same as I do. Should I fall, this family is yours and you must protect them. Watch at the western wall for our messenger. When he arrives, he'll be racing ahead of either the bloodthirsty Persians or a triumphant Greek army. If we've lost—and Alexandros, make no mistake, we will fight until the last spurt of our hearts' blood—you must take your mother and sisters and flee through the eastern gate. Run far and fast." Alexandros opened his mouth to object, but his father only shook his head and said, "The servants will give you a sword when you return home. Use it well, my son."

His father gripped Alexandros's forearm and looked into his eyes, watching him for a long time. Then he hurried to join the line of men disappearing through the western gate.

That was three days ago. Alexandros can't bear to stay in his home. His mother directs the servants in packing the valuables, which he sees as an insult to the men on the field. Does she think so little of them? Is she so certain they will die? His elder sister speeds around the house, eyes red, helping the servants. His younger sisters barely know what is happening.

Everywhere it is the same. People packing. People weeping. Old men sitting with swords on their laps. Young men running from house to house or standing on the walls or pestering the few adult men who guard the gate.

Alexandros walks along the western wall, running his palm over the rough stones. Sweat runs down his back. The road stands clear and silent, as it has for three days, the only traveler the occasional bird pecking at the dirt. Heat waves shimmer in the distance, like curtains made of air.

But then he spies the faintest whisper of dust on the road. He leans against the stone, the rough bite of it on his belly, his hands grabbing the outside wall, pulling himself toward the road. It is a small puff of dust. Not an army, then. A man. Running this way. The messenger!

He runs along the wall and bursts down the stairs like racing water, shouting that someone is coming. Everywhere people come to life. Some race to their homes, others toward the gate. The soldiers prepare to open it, and Alexandros is there with them, pressing against the gate, begging the men to open it.

The messenger is a black speck in the distance but rapidly growing larger. He stumbles and almost falls. His legs can barely hold him. One of the soldiers says, "He is running too fast. Pushing himself to his limits. That can only be a man with an enemy at his heels."

Soon Alexandros can see the messenger himself. He has thrown off anything that would weigh him down—no armor or sword. He runs in his toga and sandals. He is covered in dust and sweat and clotted blood, his toga stained dark as wine. "Another ill omen," a soldier says, yanking the rope that opens the gate.

The messenger collapses inside the walls, and the gate falls shut. His chest heaves, and he gasps for air. He tries to speak, but his lips and mouth are cracked by the sun, and the words are unintelligible, the sounds of the barbarians. They bring him a cup of water and press it to his lips. He drinks deeply, and they help him to his feet. "The Persians," he says, "outnumbered our men three to one. The men of this city fought bravely. You should be proud of their good service and valiant fight."

Alexandros feels his heart drop. No. May it not be. He mentally plans his route through the city toward home. How quickly can he get his family out the eastern gate? Will it be choked with others abandoning the city? His hand twitches. Soon he will be carrying a sword on the open road.

The messenger clears his throat and throws back another cup of water. "Yes, we fought valiantly, my friends. We won! We won! We defeated the Persians!"

A monstrous cheer unlike anything Alexandros has ever heard rises up as if from the entire city. Alexandros is amazed to find his own voice roaring alongside those of the other people in the crowd. The messenger is shouting more details from the battle, but no one can hear him. The people are leaping and screaming praise and weeping and falling into one another's arms. People shoot out along the city streets, calling the news to everyone. People begin to shout out names of loved ones, and the messenger calls back their status: alive, wounded, dead, a great hero of the battle, unknown.

Alexandros shouts his father's name over and over, waiting for the messenger to hear him. At last, the messenger turns to Alexandros, grinning, and says, "Alive! Alive and headed for home, a hero."

Alexandros leaps to his feet and runs for home, running so fast that the wind pulls tears from his eyes. He bursts into the house and swings his sister in a circle, laughing, and falls against his mother's chest. "We're saved!" he shouts. She grabs his cheeks and turns his face toward hers, and he joyously tells her the good news, shouts it to her over and over. "We're saved, and Father is alive."

What Is the Gospel?

We love to talk about the "gospel." The number of books written in the last few years with the word *gospel* in the title is enormous. You can find books to help you center your marriage in the gospel, to teach you gospel-centered parenting techniques, to teach you about the importance of the gospel or the definition of the gospel or how to be a man or a woman according to the gospel. We repeat the word like a mantra. We have coalitions and committees and seminaries centered around the gospel.

But the word *gospel* never appears in the Bible. Of course, we refer to the first four books of the New Testament as "Gospels" (the Gospels of Matthew, Mark, Luke, and John), but the word itself comes from Middle English. It has lost meaning to modern English speakers, but the original words *god spel* meant simply "good news" or "good story."

For speakers of Middle English, this was a good, direct translation of the Greek word *euangelion*, which means "good news." This was a secular term in Greek society, originally used in military matters. A messenger would run back from the front lines bringing (hopefully) the *evangel*, the good news about a conquering king, a success in battle, a victory over superior forces. Over time, the word started being used in family situations as well. The good news about Mom's doctor's appointment. The good news about a brother's advancement at work. The good news of a granddaughter being born. The one who brought the good news, the messenger, was the *evangelist*.

I'm not sure why we've latched onto the word *gospel* rather than simply translating the Greek: good news. One side effect of this choice has been that we've dressed the good news in religious clothing. Those outside the church, those who should be most interested in hearing some good news, don't realize that's what we're talking about. Imagine a conversation in which you sit down beside a stranger and say, "I want to tell you the gospel of Jesus Christ." What would they say? It would depend on the person, of course, but it's not hard to imagine them immediately dismissing us and our religious jargon. Now imagine walking up to someone and saying, "I want to tell you the good news about Jesus." Maybe they would still walk away without listening. I've tried this myself, and sometimes I get the response, "What? There's *good* news about Jesus?"

We've become so adept at telling people what they should believe and how they should act and placing that all in a brightly colored package that we call "Christianity" or "gospel" or "church" that we've missed the fact that there are people who do not realize that the news about Jesus is good. They think the gospel is about obligation, rules, responsibilities, giving things up, repenting of sins, going to services on Sunday, trying not to curse, and not eating chocolate at Lent.

Maybe some of those things are the good news, or at least part of it. But the core message is something different. Sometimes we share the good news in a strange way, focusing on things that are not central to it. It's like Alexandros running home and shouting to his family, "I hope you made your beds and cleaned the kitchen and are making something good for dinner because Father is coming home." The good news is buried in there somewhere along with the list of all the things that need to be done.

So what is the good news, exactly? If someone ran for two days from the battle lines and collapsed at the city gate, what would their first few sentences be after gulping down a cup of cool water?

For many followers of Jesus, the go-to Bible passage on this question is 1 Corinthians 15:1–5.

> Now, brothers and sisters, I want to remind you of the gospel I preached to you, which you received and on which you have taken your stand. By this gospel you are saved, if you hold firmly to the word I preached to you. Otherwise, you have believed in vain. For what I received I passed on to you as of first importance: that Christ died for our sins according to the Scriptures, that he was buried, that he was raised on the third day according to the Scriptures, and that he appeared to Cephas, and then to the Twelve.

And on it goes, telling us about all the people who saw Jesus after his resurrection.

When many of us share the good news with someone, it boils down to these points:

Jesus died for our sins.

He was buried.

He rose again.

He appeared to others (another way of saying, "This story is true").

Because of this we can be saved.

"Jesus died for our sins and rose again on the third day so that we might experience God's salvation."

Is this the gospel?

Well, yes. Certainly Paul (who wrote 1 Corinthians) thinks it's a fine definition and refers to it explicitly as the good news that he preached to the Corinthians. It's a story about what Jesus has done for us and how we can experience personal salvation as a result.

So that settles that.

The Gospel Test

Every once in a while, I'll attend a church service, or go to a Christian movie, or read a Christian book, and afterward, when I ask other believers for their thoughts, I'll hear comments like this: "It is a good book, I guess, but it doesn't really present the gospel." I even heard someone say once that a particular book of the Bible isn't that great because it doesn't clearly present the gospel. It's as if there are two criteria we use to critique a talk, a movie, or a book that purports to be Christian.

First: Is it good? Did I like it?

Second: Does it present the gospel clearly?

And if it was a wonderful, amazing talk or movie or book that doesn't "present the gospel clearly," then it has failed the test. The gospel test. It's of limited worth at best. Or, at least, that's how we talk sometimes.

Here are three (true) statements found in Scripture. There's no question that they're good and worthwhile statements that reveal something about God. The question is whether they are the "gospel." So ask yourself this: If someone shared the content listed below with someone who didn't know Jesus and then told you, "I shared the gospel," would you agree or disagree?

1. Jesus is the Messiah.
2. Jesus is descended from King David.
3. The Sermon on the Mount is the good news.

Clearly, none of these statements on its own passes the 1 Corinthians "gospel test." *Maybe* number one does, if you do a really good job explaining what *Messiah* means. I think it's safe to say that if our definition of the gospel is "Jesus died for our sins and rose again so that we can be saved," none of these three statements can be described as the gospel. They are not sufficient.

Good. I'm glad that's settled.

Except that Acts 5:42 says that every day, whether in the temple or in their homes, the followers of Jesus never stopped teaching and sharing the good news that "Jesus is the Messiah." They never stopped sharing the good news. The gospel. What gospel did they share? The gospel defined as "Jesus is the Messiah."[1]

At first you might think that's not a big deal. If we parse out what "Messiah" means, we might come up with something similar to the 1 Corinthians definition. Jesus is the Chosen One of God sent to bring hope and healing and restoration to the human race. How did he accomplish that? By dying in our place and rising from the dead. So because he is the Messiah, we can find personal salvation and be connected to God. I guess if we say it that way, "Jesus is the Messiah" might pass the 1 Corinthians gospel test. Maybe it's shorthand for the more detailed version of what we believe the gospel to be.

How about "Jesus is descended from King David"? No way. Not even close. It's not mentioned in 1 Corinthians 15, and while it's an interesting piece of trivia about Jesus's royal bloodline, it's not the gospel. Except that 2 Timothy 2:8–9 says, "Remember Jesus Christ, raised from the dead, descended from David. This is my gospel, for which I am suffering even to the point of being chained like a criminal. But God's word is not chained."

So Paul's good news includes not only that Jesus is the Messiah but also that he is David's great-great-great-lots-of-greats grandson. So I guess that's part of the gospel too. We better go back and rewrite some of our gospel tracts to say, "We forgot to add that Jesus is descended from David."

OK, but what about the third example, that the Sermon on the Mount is the good news? The sermon never mentions Jesus being the Messiah. (In fact, in other places Jesus rebuked demons who tried to share that particular bit of the gospel.) It never mentions that Jesus would die or rise again from the dead, and it never mentions our personal salvation as such. Can it be the gospel?

Let's look for a moment at the Gospel of Matthew. It starts with a genealogy (essentially, that Jesus is descended from King David). In chapter 2, Jesus is properly respected as a king. In chapter 3, John the Baptist says that Jesus is the Messiah sent by God, and in chapter 4, Jesus is tempted by the evil one. And then in Matthew 4:23, it says this: "Jesus went throughout Galilee, teaching in their synagogues, *proclaiming the good news of the kingdom*, and healing every disease and sickness." What was the good news (gospel) that Jesus was preaching?

Matthew spends three chapters writing out the answer to that question. In Matthew 5–7, Jesus gives us a gospel presentation, and if you read it through that lens, I think you'll find it incredibly fascinating. It's the good news about the coming kingdom, where the poor own the kingdom and the mourning are comforted and the pure in heart see God. This is the good news, and it doesn't match 1 Corinthians 15 at all.

Why didn't Jesus teach the same gospel?

The Gospel of the Kingdom and the Gospel of Jesus

Jesus often taught the good news of the coming kingdom, when God's reign on earth will spread and his will will be done "on earth as in heaven." Much of this good news has to do with the transformation of culture, the re-creation of the world, the justice that will come, the broken things that will be made whole. The bringing about of that kingdom is a key piece of the good news of Jesus, and he is, of course, the King of that kingdom. The good news of the kingdom and the good news of Jesus go together. Acts 8:12 talks about Philip sharing the "good news of the kingdom of God and the name of Jesus Christ."

The good news about Jesus is partly that Jesus is God, that he died for our sins, that he rose again, and that because of those things we can experience salvation. These are undoubtedly parts of the gospel.

But the transformation of all creation is part of the gospel too. The coming government that Christ will rule is part of the gospel. Scripture occasionally talks about the good news purely in the sense of the plan of salvation for human beings. But the vast majority of the time, the good news is directly related to some revelation of God's character. The good news is less "you can be saved" and more "there is a God who loves you enough to save you." Humanity's salvation results from God's character.

Also, there's a reason that the books of Matthew, Mark, Luke, and John are called the Gospels. Every word of those books is part of the good news of Jesus. Matthew starts with the genealogies, and that's the gospel. Mark starts with a prophecy from Isaiah and refers to it as the good news—that there will be one preparing the way for the Messiah. Luke starts with the story of an old priest who sees an angel and is told his son will prepare the way for the Lord. John starts with a philosophical discussion of Jesus as the Word who is God and dwells with God and made all things.

All of this is the gospel. The story of Jesus is the good news— the good news about God; the good news about the kingdom (it's here and it's coming); the good news about Jesus being the Messiah, descended from David, descended from Adam, Son of God, and his death, burial, and resurrection; the good news about our salvation; and the good news about the re-creation of the world.

"God is light; in him there is no darkness at all" (1 John 1:5). That is the gospel.

Jesus came to baptize with fire. That is the gospel.

Jesus speaking to an outcast woman at a well. Jesus caring for his mother from the cross. Jesus telling God that he does not want to die if there is another way. Jesus letting the little children come to him. All these stories are the gospel too.

The good news is larger than a handful of theological statements. The "full gospel" can't be presented in fifteen minutes or in a sermon or in a series of sermons. Every new understanding we gain about the person and character of Jesus is the good news, and he is an infinite being. The work of eternity will be learning the extent of the beautiful good news of Jesus.

Yes, the first words of a messenger at the city gate may well be, "Jesus, the Christ, died on a cross and rose from the dead for our salvation." But there are more words to come after that, many more, an eternal stream of living water that flows from the throne of God and fills the whole earth.

2

The Origin of Fire

Theo,

Everything on earth has a temperature at which it bursts into flames. Wood, for example, combusts at 572° Fahrenheit.

Heat. Oxygen. Fuel. Put those three things together and you have the makings of a fire that will sweep through forests and grasslands and cities.

It had been fifty days. A month and three weeks, give or take. That's how long it had been since they had seen the Teacher, Jesus, beaten with nightsticks, slung up on a tree, hung and murdered by a mob. It had all started on a Thursday night when the sheriff's men arrested Jesus during a prayer meeting. By Friday at nine he was on the tree, people hurling filth and insults at him, and by three in the afternoon he was dead. They lowered his body onto a sheet, put him in the back of Joe's SUV, and buried him with dignity in a crypt.

Three days. They spent three days grieving, hiding, huddling together in secret, sure that the authorities would burst in and arrest them all, drag them into the public square, put them on trial, and execute them. Men, women, children, scattered and afraid. Until the women came bursting into the room shouting their story. They had seen Jesus—alive. The other Jesus followers could scarcely believe it, but then more people saw him, saw angels, heard from one another that Jesus had returned—not as a ghost but as flesh and blood.

Forty days. That's how long the still-living Jesus taught them. Over and over, his new teaching came back to this theme: tell other people. Share your story. Tell the whole world, every nation, all your neighbors. Let them know the good news.

Now it had been just over a week since he had flown off into heaven, and they were following his directions. They had packed themselves into the attic. That's what they called it—the attic. The upper room. It was a bit of a joke, a winking nudge to the old woman who owned the house. The mansion, really. The attic was a huge room, nicer than some of their houses. It was big enough to host a concert, and they pulled in folding chairs and rearranged couches and divans and spent time talking about the Teacher, sharing stories, praying, singing.

It did get hot up there sometimes. With 120 of them packed in the room of course it got hot. Pete got up and spoke sometimes, which felt strange. Pete, bearded and smelling of fish. Pete, the headstrong, blustering oaf. Now he seemed to be thinking of them. Watching over them. Trying to guide them. People wondered what Jesus had said to Pete before he shot into the sky, narrowly missing a jumbo jet.

They were waiting, everyone on edge, everyone's nerves frayed thin and brittle as tinder.

Then came day fifty.

I've asked them to describe this to me a hundred times.

Imagine a forest. You're sitting in the woods, lush and green. There are small animals moving about in the underbrush and green-tinted sunlight filtering through the trees. Somewhere an old log catches fire somehow. Maybe it's the sunlight, or someone has thrown a match.

There's a sound of air being sucked into it, a whoosh, and the whole woods hits the flash point. The flame moves as fast and as powerful as wind, lighting the bushes, the trees, the fallen pinecones and needles. Everything is on fire simultaneously. The air moves, hot and fast, like a wind, and you are caught in the middle of it, scalding hot air, flames, fuel. And it's spreading.

They say it was like that. One moment everyone was in the room. The next, boom! An explosion. There was a sound like wind that filled not just the attic but the entire house. What looked like flames burst into the room and rested over each person's head, and all of them began to tell the story of the Teacher.

In other languages.

I know. I was skeptical too. But they began to speak in languages they didn't know. Remember the neighborhoods most of these people grew up in. They weren't linguistic scholars. Some of them told me they didn't know what language they were speaking, just that somewhere between their brains and their tongues their story of Jesus got translated into strange new words.

Every single one of them, every person I've been able to interview, says the same thing. They were filled with a holy breath. The Holy Spirit. He spoke through them. He gave them the words.

"What did it feel like?" I asked them.

"Like being blown along by the wind," one said.

"Like catching on fire but not burning up."

"Like taking a deep breath of superheated air and exhaling beauty and wonder."

They spread from the house and out into the streets, like any wildfire would. Crowds gathered, drawn by the noise, and as any crowd does, they mocked that which they couldn't understand. Or, rather, what they could understand.

People in the crowd had come from all over the world. They could pick out their own languages from this strange group of babblers.

Chinese. Persian. Farsi. French. Greek. Everyone started to ask, "What does this possibly mean? What is this? Performance art? Some sort of military action? Some elaborate prank?"

Hecklers started shouting that they were drunk.

Pete stood up to talk to the onlookers. If the wind and fire of the Holy Spirit was the first miracle, and if everyone speaking languages they didn't know was the second, Pete standing up and talking to the crowd was the third.

He was a different man.

When I ask people to tell me the story of Pete from the moment he met the Teacher through three years of traveling together to the moment Jesus was killed and on through his resurrection and the forty days of teaching, everyone describes him the same way. Hotheaded. Pigheaded. Blockheaded. That's not even counting what Pete's brother said.

This is the man who asked Jesus to heal his mother-in-law and yet didn't believe the Teacher when he told him where to catch fish. The guy who would physically attack someone who was trying to arrest the Teacher and then curse and shout that he didn't know Jesus at the first sign that he might be arrested too. He blustered and cursed and shouted at people. He said things that made no sense. He made promises he couldn't keep. He followed the Teacher with slavish devotion and then tried to correct him.

This does not describe the man who stood up in front of the rabble.

No. Pete looked at the hecklers . . . and smiled. "Drunk?" he said. "They're not drunk. It's only nine in the morning." He laughed as if to say, *Hey, even us poor folk don't start drinking whiskey out of the fruit jar this early in the day.*

Then he started the story.

"God told us this long ago," he said. "Remember what he told Joel six hundred years ago? He said that in the last days he would pour his Spirit on human beings. On all people. He told us that our sons and daughters would teach God's truth, our young men would have visions, and our old men would dream true dreams. Men and women, he said." He gestured to the men and women behind him who were sharing their own stories in the languages of every person in the crowd. "God would pour out his own Spirit on men and women, and they would teach truth. And there would be wonders in heaven, fire and blood and smoke and signs on the earth, and the sun would go black and the moon would turn red because it was time for the glorious coming of God. And," he said, his voice cracking, "everyone who calls to God for help will be saved."

Pete never spoke this way. Never before this moment. Just days before this, Pete had been up in the attic and had suggested that they needed a replacement for Jude, who had killed himself after he betrayed the Teacher. Pete had suggested rolling dice to figure out who would get to take Jude's place. It seemed strange to think that on such an important decision Pete felt uncomfortable making a call on God's behalf, but now he was standing up there, speaking with a calm authority that shocked and amazed them. They never rolled dice to make a decision again, by the way. Not after they had breathed in the flaming presence of God.

The crowd hung on his words. The hecklers had fallen silent. The entire crowd had fallen silent. "Listen," he said. "You know about Jesus. God put his stamp of approval on the man. We knew he was from God because he did miracles right here in our town. You know this. God did miracles through him here." He pointed at the pavement in front of his feet. No one denied it. Pete went on. "He was handed over to you. To the authorities. God knew this would happen. It didn't cross his purposes. And then you did it." He ran his hand through his thick beard. "You—with the help of corrupt officials—killed him. You lynched him. Yes, it was a mob just like this one. But God undid your handiwork and brought him back to life. Death could not keep him down."

Then Pete started quoting poetry to them straight from that ancient king David. It was a poem about seeing God all around, even through wind and storm and quake. How happiness and hope spread from his heart to his mouth to his whole body because he knew that God would never allow him to rot in Hades. In fact, the poem said that the Holy One would never experience decay, ever.

Then, in a brilliant piece of literary exposition, Pete explained that the poet was not referring to himself but to Jesus, who was dead and now is alive and sitting in the presence of God, submerging his followers in the burning flame of his own Spirit. "Know this," he said. "God has made this man, Jesus, who you murdered, both ruler and the Chosen One."

When people in the crowd heard those words, many of them reached for their chests, as if someone had run them through with a sword. "What do we do then?" they shouted, not just to Pete but to anyone who would answer. And Pete and all of them said the same thing in many languages. Turn away from your evil lives. Make a public commitment to God in the name of Jesus Christ so that God will forgive all the wrong things you've done. Then God will give you this same Holy Spirit.

"Who can do this?" someone called. "Who is this for?"

You have to understand, Theo, that they were used to theological "classes." They expected the spiritual life to reflect their social life. Some people had power, and some did not. Some had money, and some did not. Some would receive forgiveness, and some would not.

Pete said, "It's for all of you. And for your children too. Anyone God calls. It's an unconditional promise. Save yourselves," he said. He kept at it for hours, trying to find the right combination of words to bring them to God. Trembling with emotion, more than once he said, "Save yourselves."

This was not the Pete they knew.

Three thousand people "saved themselves" that day, Theo. When's the last time you saw three thousand people? New Year's Eve at Time's Square? A sporting event? A mall during the holidays? Three thousand people, all of them begging to come to God and finding forgiveness.

That is the origin of fire. On day fifty, the Holy Spirit burst onto the scene.

He was the flame and the oxygen; they were the fuel. And the fire burned and spread and consumed every heart it touched.

Why "The Acts of the Apostles" Is a Terrible Title

The title "The Acts of the Apostles" or, more commonly, "The Book of Acts," was added to the book around a hundred years after it was written. It started as a letter (people wrote long letters in the olden days) to a person named Theophilus. That name means "friend of God." There are a lot of theories about this person and who he might have been or if he existed at all. Some people, for instance, say that "Theophilus" is a way of saying the letter is for any friend of God.

My favorite theory is that Theophilus was a patron of Luke and that he (Greek tense would suggest that Theophilus was most likely a man) gave Dr. Luke money to produce a work of history that would be of use to Theophilus himself and to the greater community of Jesus followers. Theophilus wanted a carefully researched document that would clarify what actually happened. He wanted interviews with the original people involved. Luke had already produced a work on the life of Christ, and this was his sequel.

As with any literary work, one question is what genre this book falls into. Is it a biography? History? Epistle (a letter)? Action thriller? You could probably make a decent argument for each of these.

Like a biography, Acts tells the story of a person (or, rather, a group of people).

Like a history, it documents a series of important events.

Like a letter, it opens with Luke addressing the recipient and explaining why he's writing.

Like an action thriller, there are car chases and plane crashes and moving speeches and heroes and villains.

I love the suggestion that Acts falls in the genre of "aretalogy." This comes from the Greek word *aretē*, which means something like "righteousness" or "right actions" or maybe even "noble character." The idea of an aretalogy is that it tells the story of a heroic person, focusing on their mighty deeds. So unlike a biography, it might never mention when or where the person was born. Unlike a history, it might completely neglect political or historical facts in order to focus on the hero. Unlike a letter, it doesn't end with farewells or focus on updates of interest to the recipient. Unlike an action thriller, there may not be a satisfying conclusion, with the hero triumphant and the enemy brought to destruction.

So why would I say that "The Acts of the Apostles" is a terrible name? If it's a book about the amazing, righteous, mighty works of the apostles, wouldn't that actually be a pretty good (if straightforward) title?

I'll start by saying this. Dr. Luke was a classically educated man. He understood Greek well. In fact, in Acts, he sometimes uses different levels of Greek to show different types of speakers. He undoubtedly understood genre and writing well and was familiar with Aristotle's theories of story and writing. Indeed, the book of Luke easily fits into an Aristotelian understanding of story. There is a clear beginning, middle, and end.

Which brings us to this question: Who is the main character in the book of Acts? The book starts by recapping what happened in Luke, a book very clearly about Jesus, the Christ. We might expect a sequel to pick up with more stories about Jesus, which it sort of does. But we jump in, mostly, to a story about Peter and the other followers of Jesus.

So is this a story about Peter? Not really. He's a major player, but he all but disappears starting in chapter 13.

Is this a story about the apostles? The definition of apostle that Peter seems to buy into is in Acts 1:21: someone who had been a part of Jesus's ministry from the very beginning, starting with his baptism by John the Baptist, and going all the way through until they witnessed his resurrection. So, to Peter at least, an apostle walked with Jesus for his three years of ministry and then saw him crucified and resurrected. But in Acts, people who were not apostles in this sense—people like Stephen, Philip, and Cornelius—show up and take over the book for a while.

Now, you could argue that they are players in the story of Paul, who becomes central in the latter half of the book. But it's interesting that, in the book of Acts (unlike in Paul's letters), Paul is rarely referred to as an apostle.[1] When Luke talks about "the apostles," he's referring most often and most clearly to those who walked with Jesus and were witnesses to his resurrection. And if it's the story of the apostles, why don't we hear more about Matthew? Or Bartholomew? Or Thomas? If we're going to call the book "The Acts of the Apostles," it might be nice to get a little story about each of them.

So is it a story about Paul? Not really. Let's even assume that in Luke's eyes Paul is an apostle in the same sense as Peter. If it's Paul's story, where is he in the first half of the book? And if it's his story, why does the book end the way it does, saying that he "remained under house arrest" for two years instead of saying (spoiler) that he was released by the authorities and then, a few years later, executed by the Roman Empire? Why didn't Luke wait to send the letter until more of Paul's story had been revealed?

So whose story is this? Who is the main character?

In most stories, certainly in traditional stories of Luke's time, the main character is the one who shows up throughout the story, beginning, middle, and end. That rules out Peter. That rules out Paul. Because of the little side jog into the story of Stephen (who is never referred to as an apostle—we might call him a deacon, but more on that later), it even rules out "the apostles."

Who shows up in the story—beginning, middle, and end?

Only one person: the Holy Spirit.

The book of Acts is not the story of the acts of the apostles. It's the story of the acts of the Holy Spirit. Every story about the apostles is actually a story of them being carried away by the Holy Spirit, of him speaking through them. *He* does mighty acts. They are vehicles for his actions. He speaks through Peter. He speaks through Stephen, and Philip, and Paul. The community of faith, the apostles, the deacons, the missionaries, the players big and small in the church—the Holy Spirit guides them throughout Acts. He leads them, speaks to them, teaches them, empowers them. This book is about, first and foremost, the righteous actions of the Holy Spirit. It's his aretalogy. It's his story.

The Story the Holy Spirit Tells

The book of Acts tells the tale of the Holy Spirit's mighty works in the early days of the church. It's actually a perfect place to start a sequel to Luke's previous book, the good news of Luke. At the end of that book, Jesus tells his followers, "Stay in the city until you have been clothed with power from on high" (24:49).

So they stay in the city for roughly ten days. Those ten days barely rate a sentence in Luke, and in Acts, one quick story tells what happens: Peter and the others find a replacement for the traitor, Judas. It is the "to be continued" of Luke and the "previously" of Acts.

Acts picks up where Luke left off. While Luke was the story of Jesus and all the things he said and did, Acts is the story of the Holy Spirit and what he does with the good news about Jesus.

What's the first thing the Holy Spirit does? He tells a story. He bursts like a mighty rushing wind into the room where Jesus's followers are gathered. He pours himself into the men and women in the room, and he begins to tell the story of Jesus through their mouths, forming their lips and tongues around strange words and strange languages.

They spill out of the home where they had been meeting, flowing out into the streets among the many foreigners who are in town, and a bewildered crowd forms, each person amazed to hear their language spoken perfectly by locals.

Men and women, young and old, preach to those who do not know Jesus. Here it is, the first church service, and here is the order of worship: everyone preaches. And the service is held in the public square. We know, by the way, that women preached in this instance. As Peter says in 2:18, quoting from the prophet Joel, "Even on my servants, both men and women, I will pour out my Spirit in those days, and they will prophesy." If women were not preaching alongside men that day, this prophecy would not have been fulfilled.

Peter finally stands before the throng and shares the Spirit's message:

> A man from Nazareth, Jesus, came from God and proved his divinity through miracles, wonders, and signs.
> He was handed over to the authorities.
> Wicked leaders conspired to murder him.
> God raised him from the dead.
> Now Jesus has been made both Lord and Christ.

It's not a theological discourse. It isn't a lengthy description of God and who he is and his character. It's not like Paul's letters, which carefully walk through theological concerns in careful, measured words. It's a story, and like many stories, it starts with the simple invitation to listen.

It's significant that the good news is first and foremost a story. Some of us may struggle with theology. Many of us don't have seminary degrees or jobs as pastors or missionaries. But every follower of Jesus has a story. It starts with "the first time I saw him" and moves from there, through highs and lows, darkness and light, storm and clear weather, until it comes to this precise moment, the moment when we are telling the story and those around the campfire listen with wonder or disbelief.

Jesus gave his followers a directive: teach everyone on earth what I taught you. But wait until the Holy Spirit comes to bring you power.

When he arrives, the Holy Spirit comes with a strategic plan, a carefully devised tool: a story that turns the whole world upside down.

"The Acts of the Apostles." I understand why someone came along and named Luke's work that. But I wonder if a better name wouldn't have been "The Holy Spirit Tells a Story."

3

Ordinary Earthquakes

I meet Brandon at the high school where he works as a track coach. He's just dismissed his team, and they're headed to their cars, sweaty and exhausted, their arms resting on their heads, their bags strapped across their chests. I ask one of the kids where the coach is, and she says, "On the track. Where else?"

The track lights have just popped on, and bugs begin to swirl in the yellow light. Brandon runs on the far side, his legs pumping in rhythmic repetition. He raises a hand to me, and in a few moments he comes around the bend toward me. "Thanks for meeting me, Coach," I say as he comes closer.

"Run with me," he shouts, not even slowing down.

I'm wearing slacks and a button-down shirt. I can't imagine going far in the loafers I'm wearing either. My bag with all my notes is slung across my shoulder. "I can't," I say.

Coach Brandon laughs at that, comes to a stop, and takes a deep breath. His chest is drenched, his white hair doused with sweat.

He points to the bleachers. "Let's sit for a minute then." He's in his late fifties, fit, with thick, muscled legs and an athlete's quick grace. I move to sit on the bottom bench, and he leaps up onto the seats and races toward the top. I convince him to come down to the center at least.

He plops down beside me and stretches his legs out in front of him. He taps the toes of his left foot against the right. "Thanks for coming out to the school, Dr. Lucas," he says.

"No problem," I say, pulling out my little arsenal of writing tools. I show him the mini-recorder and with his permission set it on the bleachers. I prefer paper and pen, so I pull those out too, touch the pen to my tongue, and write Brandon's name and the date at the top of a page. "I appreciate your making the time. Just tell me how it all happened, in your own words."

"Sure." He pushes his hair back, runs back down to grab a water bottle, and then runs back up to me. He takes a deep drink. "My legs, Doc, you wouldn't believe. I saw plenty of your kind over the years."

"You had some sort of congenital lower limb deficiency I'm told?"

"The short story is that I couldn't walk at all. I had a wheelchair, and my parents had looked into amputation or getting me fitted for prosthetics, but we didn't have any money. My father had lost his insurance just before I was born, so we were getting by on charity and our own cash."

It wasn't a new story, but it saddened me to hear it nonetheless. "There wasn't an organization that could have helped?"

"Not that I know of. My parents did what they could. I realized I could at least make some money begging. I hated it, but I made enough money that it was worth it. My parents or one of the neighbors would wheel me out to a prime location. I'd wear shorts so people could see my legs."

I look at his legs, which are chiseled muscle now. "What did they look like?"

He waves a bug away from his face. "Thin. Twisted. Like kindling. Dry sticks. The big problem was my ankles and feet. They couldn't hold any weight. I would sit like this," he says, and lays his legs in front of him. "I learned to look down at the ground, with my hand out for money. No one wants to look you in the face if they can help it. It's embarrassing for everyone. This particular day, though, I knew there was a big prayer meeting at the church, and I got dropped off there. I sat on the sidewalk right near one of the main entrances. I sat on the sidewalk because it's public property. No one can tell you to move along."

"You were worried about that?"

"Ha." He takes another healthy swig of water from his bottle. "Doc, you gotta understand that it doesn't matter why you're begging; people think you're no good. There's nothing you can say that will convince them otherwise. If you say good morning to someone when they pass, maybe one in twenty will say good morning back. One in fifty might look at you. One in a hundred might stop to really talk to you. That's what surprised me about Pete and John when they came by."

"They looked at you?"

"More than that. I was looking down at the sidewalk, doing my unspoken duty as a beggar—never look at the healthy people with the cash—when I heard a voice say, 'Look at me.' I figured someone was about to give me some money, so I looked up and saw them—one guy who looked like a teamster and another who looked like he'd been used to hard work his whole life. Blue-collar guys with big, thick arms and legs. Their arms looked almost as strong as mine."

"Commercial fishermen," I say.

"I could tell that when I first looked up. I'm waiting for them to give me some change, so I've got my hand out. Pete, he's looking in my eyes with this real intense look. He says, 'Listen, kid, I don't have any cash on me, but I'll give you what I do have.' Then he takes my right hand and pulls. He says, 'In the name of the Savior, Jesus from Nazareth, get up and walk.'"

I lean forward. This is the part I've wondered about. "What happened? Tell me exactly."

He shrugs. "First, this terrific heat poured through me. My ankles straightened out in a way I'd never seen. The weirdest thing for me, Doc, was the muscles. I hadn't been able to use my legs most of my life, and what muscles I had were puny. Like baby muscles. But I could feel them thickening . . . getting harder. By the time Pete had pulled me all the way to my feet, John helping to support me on the other side, I could stand. I balanced there, barely believing it. I took a step. Then two."

I clear my throat. "You didn't have to learn to walk, like a child?"

He shakes his head. "Pete and John, they walked on as if they had just thrown a ten-dollar bill in my hat. Like I wouldn't have questions or want to talk to them. Like it was an everyday occurrence. I started walking along beside them, and then I had this urge to, you know, to *run*. I sprinted in front of them and around the courtyard of the church, and then I came back to them and I ran up some stairs. I was amazed by the way my legs stretched out and covered the ground, how one foot went out and the other swung ahead when it was settled. I jumped two steps at a time and then three and then I turned around on the stairs and jumped five of them, right down to the bottom! I started racing around, jumping, leaping, twirling, laughing!"

"Did you say anything? Did you talk to Pete and John?"

"I kept saying over and over, 'Thank you, God! Thank you, God!' No one could believe it. Plenty of people had seen me over the years, Doc. Lots of people knew me or my family. Now they were all shouting at me, asking what had happened, how my legs had grown strong. I ran over to Pete and John. They were trying to get away from me, but I held on to them both in the most tremendous bear hug."

I try to picture it. Pete has never been a man I would describe as cuddly. "How did they respond?"

He laughs. "Pete stood there, awkward as a statue. John hugged me back and said, 'God loves you, little child. He has always loved you.' A crowd formed, and everyone was talking, shouting in amazement and wonder. They had so many questions.

"Finally, Pete looked at them and said, 'Why are you surprised by this?'"

I had to laugh at that. Pete has always been a simple man. He has seen astonishing things over the years, which he has often taken in stride. Once something becomes established fact to him, he finds it inconceivable that others haven't figured it out. "I can hear him saying that."

Brandon stands up, stretching his legs. "He told them that they were ridiculous to think that the whole thing was his and John's doing. He told them it was Jesus, the author of life himself, who they had killed. We had killed. God had brought him back to life though. He said he knew we had done it in ignorance, and now was the time to turn away from our evil lives and accept the blessing of God: an escape from our evil ways."

Earthquake Weather

There's a phenomenon called "earthquake weather." Supposedly, there are signs that warn that an earthquake is about to happen. If you're paying attention, you might notice that birds have fallen silent when they should be singing, or vice versa. The air seems heavy. There's not a cat anywhere, and dogs howl mournfully. Those on the coast might notice strange, deep-water fish washing up on the shore. In Japan and California, the rare oarfish swims past fishermen, and they are startled to see such a thing in shallow waters.

These events are a warning of things to come.

Soon the religious and political leaders will be shouting that these early followers of Jesus have turned the world upside down, but for now there's a response of wonder and amazement. The followers of Jesus seem almost surprised by this. In this story, Peter even asks everyone what the big deal is. "Why does this surprise you?" he asks (Acts 3:12), as if it's an everyday occurrence, as if the man born unable to walk had been in a waiting room and Peter had just now gotten around to healing his legs.

I imagine Peter and John rifling through their pockets, looking for loose change, and Peter saying, "You know what, pal? I don't have any cash, but I guess I could fix your legs for you." No big deal. Just another day as a follower of Jesus.

When the crowds form, trying to figure out what has happened, Peter starts preaching again. There are two particularly beautiful phrases in Acts 3. One is "You killed the author of life, but God raised him from the dead" (v. 15). It's an amazing, poetic sentiment to tell people that they had snuffed out the life of the one who authored life and, it seems to me, evidence of the Holy Spirit speaking through Peter, who wasn't one for flights of verbal fancy. It's a moment when Peter clearly equates Jesus with God. Jesus is the one who created life, designed it. Peter drives home the monstrous nature of our decision to murder him—to try to take life from the one who invented it.

Then Peter tells them to repent and turn to God "so that your sins may be wiped out, that times of refreshing may come from the Lord," and that he will send them their savior, Jesus, who has been "appointed for you" (3:19–20).

I love this description. My whole life I've been told to repent so my sins can be forgiven. For me, that has sometimes meant seeing the entire process as a transaction between a sinner and the sinned-upon, the equivalent of apologizing for speaking angrily to a sibling or for wrecking a friend's car. But the way Peter (and the Holy Spirit) says it here causes me to pause and reflect. He talks about my sins being "wiped out." Done away with. Not just forgiven but destroyed. And unlike the "forgiveness" metaphor, it doesn't end with us shaking hands and agreeing that we can be friends again. Rather, Peter says that when our sins are wiped out, we'll experience a time of refreshment. Peace. Life. Rest. All those things in the presence of our dear Jesus.

In fact, Peter goes on to say that Jesus was sent to *bless* us. The Greek word for "bless" is similar to the English word for "happy." He's saying that Jesus was sent to us to bring us happiness, a startling claim after accusing his listeners of murder. More startling for me is the way that Jesus blesses us: by turning each of us from our wicked ways (3:26).

I have this habit of clutching onto my sin. God can seem petty as he removes things from my life, demanding that I fall in line with a moral code that seems strange, or difficult, or even impossible. But Peter tells us that God wants to move us away from our sinful habits because to give those things up will result in great happiness for us. With blessing. That's an amazing thought.

This speech in Acts 3 is undoubtedly a truncated version. Peter and John show up for prayer at the temple at three in the afternoon. While they're talking to the crowd, telling them about Jesus, the priests in charge of security show up and tell them that they're going to hold them for the night because it's evening now and the religious leaders aren't in session anymore and therefore can't make a judgment on their teaching. Peter and John were teaching people for at least a few hours before they were arrested by the temple guards (think in-house security).

For their part, the religious leaders have no idea what to do. They aren't pleased that Peter and John are teaching that Jesus came back from the dead, but they can't deny the miracle of the lame man's sudden ability to walk, run, leap, and praise God.

They command Peter and John to keep things quiet about Jesus from now on, but Peter and John say they have to obey God rather than human authority (a concept we'll return to in a later chapter).

Notice this too: in Acts 4:13, it says that the religious leaders were "astonished" that "unschooled, ordinary men" showed such bravery in their answers to the religious council. They "took note" that they had been with Jesus. "Unschooled" in the Jewish context would probably be the equivalent today of us saying that they hadn't had formal training in theology. They hadn't been to seminary. We know, at least, that most of the Twelve were laymen and wouldn't have been expected to hold their own in a theological discourse with the "professionals."

This is an important insight into the character of the Jesus followers. We should take note as well. Those who have been with Jesus—ordinary people—become astonishing. Something about the proximity to the author of life creates people who are unexpectedly courageous, inexplicably insightful. Their courage and insight weren't the result of hard work and study (wonderful things, both) but of nearness to the Savior who was given to them when they repented. Their sins were wiped out, and they were blessed with the refreshing presence of Jesus.

Standing beside them throughout is the man whose withered legs have gone from fragile sticks to living trees (4:14). He was arrested alongside them, apparently. The leaders threaten them multiple times, trying to elicit a promise of silence from Peter and John. When Peter and John return to the other followers of Jesus, they pray for the exact opposite: great boldness to preach and continued miracles.

This is all the beginning of a rumbling at the core of the world. Tectonic plates are shifting, rubbing against one another. An earthquake is coming.

Shaken

"I went back with them, of course," Brandon says. "I didn't want them to leave, even after a night in jail together, and so I followed them back to the other believers."

"They invited you to go with them?" I ask.

"It wouldn't matter if they did or not. I was going with them." He's doing toe touches now. "I was surprised by the people there. They weren't what I expected. No one famous. No one with tons of education. A few rich people, but mostly people, well, like me. Ordinary. Normal."

I nod my head. The movement started at the bottom of society. That was the way of the Teacher too. He spoke to the ordinary people. The rich and the famous came to him, not the other way around. Not often, at least. "How did they respond to the threats from the religious leaders?"

Brandon bounces on the balls of his feet and points at me. "That's the thing, right? They're these ordinary people. Pete and John have just been threatened by some of the most influential people in our society. Guess what all the people did when Pete and John tell them about it."

"I suppose they were afraid."

"Could be. But they all started praying. They really believed that the answer was God, not a lawsuit or a petition or a council meeting. They quoted from the Bible, saying that all the plans of powerful nations don't matter when they're up against God himself. Then they asked God to make them bolder. They asked him to keep healing people. It was an amazing response."

"They aren't ordinary people at all, are they?"

"Oh yes, they are. On their own they are the most common, ordinary people. They're people like me, Doc. High school teachers and architects and stay-at-home parents and editors and longshoremen and airline attendants. It's not the people who are extraordinary. It's what's inside them."

"What? Courage?"

Brandon shakes his head. "I said it wrong, Doc. It's *who's* inside them. The Holy Spirit." He grins at me. "Watch this." He starts to pound his feet rhythmically on the bench we're sitting on. He's stomping, over and over. He's jumping up and down, and the metal under me is bouncing.

"What are you doing?"

"When we were praying, it was like a sporting event."

"What was?"

He stops jumping. "That crackling feeling in the air. They're all praying for boldness, and there's this excitement. They start talking about the miracles. I reach down and feel my legs, and they're solid. Pure muscle. There's a rumbling sound, low and quiet at first, but as we keep praying, it's getting stronger. Stronger and stronger, building, growing, getting louder. The whole place starts to shake, as if an entire stadium full of people are stomping in time to a chant. Dust is falling from the ceiling, and then it's like I breathed a chest full of the purest oxygen. My lungs are on fire, and I'm yelling alongside every person in there, and we spill out into the streets and start telling people the good news about Jesus."

Brandon is shaking now, his muscles twitching. The memory of the event is strong for him, clearly. I ask him how he feels.

"It's time to run, Doc," he says. He pulls me to my feet. "Come on, just a few laps."

"I don't have the right shoes," I say.

He bends down and unlaces his. "We'll run barefoot if we have to."

"OK," I say, tucking my notepad into my bag. "OK, OK." I unlace my shoes and set my bag down on the bleachers.

Brandon leaps down the stairs like a newly shorn sheep. When I get to the bottom, we run. We run until I can't breathe and the sweat drenches my aching chest. I lay on my back in the center of the track, and Brandon circles around, again and again, running, leaping, praising God.

4

Dead Money

"I feel uncomfortable talking about this," Joseph says. We're walking through the Rescue Center, a series of apartments designed for people in the community who have fallen on hard times or don't have much money.

"Everyone does," I say. "But the story is important. I don't think we should hide anything."

"Who's hiding anything?" Joseph pushes his thick, black glasses up his nose. "Here's my room."

He unlocks the door and steps aside. There's a simple single bed with a blue comforter. His Bible is on the bedside table alongside a small lamp. He has his own bathroom and a short shelf of books. There's a hot plate on a small counter by the closet. His suits are hung in the closet, but they are simple too. "It's nice," I say. It's a dorm room.

Joseph nods. "We have larger places for families and couples. I don't need a kitchenette. I'm at work for most meals."

I lean on the windowsill. "How long have you been living here?"

"You know the answer to that," Joseph says. He sets his briefcase down beside the bed. He loosens his tie and hangs it. "I wish you didn't, but you do."

"Like I said, I don't think we should hide anything."

Joseph blushes. "It's just that people always talk about my money, and I wish they wouldn't."

It's true that people talk about his money. Joseph's father left him with a successful import and export business and a net worth of several million dollars. At one time, he lived a lavish life complete with a mansion, swimming pools, tennis courts, and sports cars. People also talk about his ability to give a hand on the shoulder, a kind word, or a bit of help at just the moment when you most need it. In fact, the Twelve gave him the nickname "the Encourager." It's no surprise. If you spent a week in the community, you'd know who they were talking about. "You basically built this place, though, right?"

Joseph shakes his head again. "No, no, no." He motions for me to get up. "Come on, I have to show you something." We leave his room, and he locks the door behind me. "You ask good questions," he says, the Encourager encouraging me during our little interview. "I did put a chunk of the original money down," he says as I follow him down the hallway.

"I heard about that." Joseph is a man of understatement. He sold his mansion and brought the money in cash to the Twelve. He set multiple briefcases at their feet and suggested that they use the money to build a place for the poorest among them. Then he slept on people's couches until the place was built and Pete made him move in there too. "How did people respond?"

Joseph sighs. "I didn't expect that, honestly, Dr. Lucas. I didn't want all that attention."

"Then why bring millions of dollars in cash and give it to the Twelve?"

"I just thought it would be easier. I knew they didn't have a checking account. We hadn't organized as a 501(c)(3) or even an LLC. We were a bunch of people who had something in common . . . this amazing connection to God. We hadn't figured out how to deal with everything else yet. Did you talk to someone about what happened with the Hispanic community?"

"Oh yes, I've heard about that. I'll do some interviews and get the whole story."

Joseph punches me in the arm. "I thought so. You don't want to leave the bad stuff out, right?"

"Right. So you brought all that cash because you thought it would be the easiest way to give them the money?"

Joseph shrugs. "Despite what you see on television, giant checks aren't practical."

"You were surprised by people's response?"

"Yes. People started calling me 'the Encourager,' which is kind of them but also embarrassing. Then other people started selling their houses and property. They would bring it to the Twelve, just like I did. The funny thing is no one even asked for money. We all saw that there were people in need."

Joseph stops by a small table that's been set up in a hallway. There are fresh flowers in the vase, and he leans over to smell them. He makes room for me, and I smell them too. "How did you know that?"

"Well, we often ate together, for instance. We had a big dinner one night where everyone brought food, and we were all sharing. There was a man next to me from another country. He had been in town for the festival and had heard about the Teacher from someone in the square. I asked him if he missed his home country, and he said, 'Here we have food.' He didn't speak great English. Before he joined us, he had nothing. Three kids, a wife, all of them living out of a twenty-year-old station wagon held together with duct tape and dust. I looked at our potluck dinner and thought, *Why can't we do the same thing with our money that we did tonight with the food?* We all brought what we had, and there was enough for everyone. It didn't make any sense for me to be in a house so big that I needed a golf cart to get from my bedroom to the kitchen."

I raise my eyebrows. "You drove a golf cart inside your house?"

He waves my question away. "I only did that once. My mother was not a fan of the idea." He pushes a glass door open, and we exit into a courtyard. There's a fountain in the middle, a patch of grass, and a few benches. He leads me to the fountain and points down at the brickwork. Each brick has a name etched into it. There are about thirty of them. "I thought it would be nice to remember all the people who gave money to build the Rescue Center."

I read through the list, writing down a few names. "I don't see your name, Joseph."

He shrugs. "I get enough attention already."

There's a wrought iron table with two iron chairs pulled up to the sides. Joseph offers me a seat and pulls up across from me. There's a chess set on the table, and he idly sets the pieces up for a game. "You're stalling," I say. When the pieces are set, I move a pawn into the center of the board. "What about the other two? Are their names on the fountain?"

Joseph pushes a pawn across the board. "You need to understand that Mercy and Bella were good people. I'd known them most of my life. They were at all the charity galas. They gave money to third world countries and paid for wells and supported orphans. They used their money for other people."

I stop and consider Joseph more carefully. He's not looking at the board. His eyes are unfocused, looking at me over the top of his glasses. "They were your friends?"

He shrugs. "My parents' friends. They came over to the house occasionally. They gave me gifts on my birthday. Lavish gifts, usually."

"They sound generous."

Joseph narrows his eyes. "Yes. They always did seem generous." There's a slight emphasis on the word *seem*.

"Why do you say it like that?"

Joseph purses his lips and leans back in his chair. A bird is chirping in one of the trees in the courtyard. He looks for it in the branches, but when he can't find it, he turns back to me. "My parents gave a lot of money too, Dr. Lucas."

"I'm sure they did."

"It wasn't until after my father's death that I found out how much money they had donated to various causes. Cancer research. Religious charities. They had put a few kids through college. Helped a series of drug addicts get back on their feet after rehab. There was a lengthy list."

I pick up one of the knights. The carving on its long snout looks like it was done by hand. As I look more carefully at the pieces, I can tell it isn't a cheap set. The knight feels heavy in my hand. Marble, maybe. "You had no idea about it until your father died though."

"As I started thinking about it, I remembered a few things. Him stopping to buy someone else's gas. He used to give money to homeless people begging in the center of the street. He always saw people, not their status. He didn't see poor people or rich people. He saw people in need, and he found ways to meet those needs."

I flip open my notebook and scribble a few lines. "So you're saying that your parents and Mercy and Bella weren't so different then."

Joseph pinches his glasses by the bridge and rubs the lenses against his shirt. "I'm saying that I had no idea who my parents gave money to or how much. But somehow I knew all about Mercy and Bella's charitable giving. I knew which fund-raising dinners they had been to, who the speakers had been, how much they had pledged, and what good works would come from it. It never seemed like bragging. It would start with a story they had heard at the dinner that was so *compelling* that they couldn't stop themselves from giving to those war orphans. They paid to build three schools. Like that."

"You don't think they liked helping those people?"

"Helping people is gratifying, Doctor. Surely a medical professional like yourself understands that. I'm sure they enjoyed it. But they also enjoyed the attention. Human beings are creatures of mixed motivations."

"Do you think what happened between them and the Twelve was a result of mixed motivations?"

Joseph snorts. He moves his pawn back into place. He stands up and paces around the courtyard. "The strangest thing to me is that Mercy and Bella didn't come together. I was with the Twelve at the time. A lot of us were. It was during a celebration meeting. We were singing and praying, and Mercy came in the back and came right up to the front of the room carrying several sacks of money."

"Still no checking account, huh?"

Joseph rolls his eyes. "I wish I had written a check. It had become almost a tradition that people would bring the money in cash. Mercy brought his money up and laid it down in front of the Twelve and said something like, 'Praise God! Bella and I have sold our ranch property down south, and here's all the money. Do with it as you see fit.' People clapped him on the back and shook his hand. Everyone cheered."

"Not everyone," I say.

Joseph acknowledges this with a nod. "Pete stood up and walked over to Mercy, I thought to shake his hand. I was cheering along with the rest of them."

"Why was everyone cheering? Hadn't this happened multiple times now?"

He leans against the wall. "It's just that every time it happened it was like a reminder that we were in this together. Whatever we had lost by coming into this community, whatever people said about us outside, whatever hardships we faced, at least we were together. Every gift was a reminder of how unique this society was. It was a reminder that God loved us and that we loved each other." He scratches his chin. "It was beautiful."

"OK. Mercy brings in the money, everyone cheers, and Pete comes over to shake hands."

"He didn't shake his hand. I was standing near Mercy by then. I wanted to give him a hug. One of the others—I don't remember who—looked at the sacks of money and said, 'That's amazing that you sold your entire ranch and that you're giving all the money to the people.' Mercy beamed at that. He actually turned and smiled at us, and we were all smiling along with him.

"Pete, though, moved through the crowd to stand in front of us. Mercy put his hand out, and Pete said, 'Mercy, how have you become so controlled by the adversary that you have lied to the Holy Spirit? You kept some of the money for yourself, as is your right. It was your land. When you sold the land, it was your money. Why did you lie? You've lied not only to this community but also to God himself.'"

Joseph's face is still as stone. I don't say anything. He's staring at the ground, his mouth slightly open. I'm about to ask him if he's OK when he starts to talk again. "Mercy's face," he says, "went from a grin into this frozen smile. The corners of his mouth faded downward. When Pete finished talking, Mercy wobbled, like a top, and then fell. Several of us tried to catch him, but he collapsed on the ground. I felt for a pulse, but he was already cold. His color had begun to change. There was nothing left in him. He was gone."

"What did you do?"

"Some young men went and found a sheet. They rolled his body onto it and carried him out. To the funeral parlor, I suppose. As you can imagine, the party was over. No more songs. No more dancing. Most everyone left. I stayed with the Twelve."

"How did people feel? Sad?"

"Not at that moment. Shocked, I'd say. The way people walked out of the room it was like they were in a trance. Scared too. Thus far it had been all miracles and singing and a few hardships followed by more miracles and singing. Suddenly God seemed terrifying."

"Were the Twelve terrified?"

Joseph sits down again. He closes his eyes and rubs the bridge of his nose. "No. I remember thinking maybe they had spent enough time with the Teacher not to be frightened by such things. It was another kind of miracle. A terrible, horrible miracle. God had revealed himself not just as the giver of life but also as the sustainer, and he had chosen to let Mercy die. Pete seemed angry but also sad. Disappointed. You've probably disappointed your parents. It was almost like that. Furious that Mercy had lied and saddened by the consequences of it."

Joseph picks up a chess piece and says quietly, "This was my father's board once, Dr. Lucas. I couldn't bring myself to sell it. I've left it here, in the courtyard, thinking some of the others might like to play, but no one does. I've often wondered if I should sell it and give the money to the assembly."

The base of each piece looks to have been painted with gold. I pick up the queen and study her. Ivory? Marble? This board is likely worth a few thousand dollars. "Do you think it's sinful to keep it?"

Joseph clears his throat. "No. It's mine. If someone needed the money, I would hand it over. No one in the community begrudges me it." He knocks a pawn over. "That's the saddest thing about this story."

"What happened when Bella came?"

Joseph sighs. "I remember that she looked beautiful. She had a dress perfectly tailored to her. She had done her hair. She walked in, confident and smiling. She hesitated when she saw the room was mostly empty. Her head kept tracking from side to side; no doubt she was looking for Mercy. She walked over to Pete, and we were all silent. Pete showed her the money and asked her if it was the full amount they had received. She said yes, that she had counted the money herself after they made the sale.

"Pete listened to her carefully. I could tell he wished she had said something different. He said, 'Bella, why have you and your husband formed a conspiracy against God? Did you honestly think you could lie to him and get away with it?' Her eyes flickered to the side, looking for Mercy again. 'Your husband is dead,' Pete said. We could hear the young men who had taken her husband out talking to one another as they came down the hallway. 'That's the sound of the men who buried him coming in the door.' As he said it, Bella crumpled. Her head hit the ground hard when she fell, and one leg bent under her in a position I knew wasn't for the living. They wrapped her up and took her away too."

Joseph has stood up, and he has his back to me. "I guess you didn't put their names on the fountain then," I say, trying to make a small joke to lighten the mood.

When Joseph turns to me, his face is wet with tears. He doesn't wipe them. He comes to me, takes me by the arm, and pulls me to the fountain. He begins to point at names. "Do you know how much he gave? Or her? Or them? How about this one?"

"I have no idea," I say. "I don't know."

He wipes the tears from his face. "Because it doesn't matter. Who cares how much someone gave? They could have had their names on the fountain if they wanted to. They could have given ten dollars and had their names on the fountain."

He wipes his eyes again and sighs. He looks at his watch. "Dinnertime, Doctor." He puts his hand on my shoulder. "Don't mention the chess set to anyone," he says. We walk to dinner together. Everyone has brought some food . . . small dishes and large, things lovingly made at home, things generously purchased from the grocery store. We eat, and after the meal there are leftovers for people to take home if they wish.

A Troubling Story of God at Work

Many theologians have debated the story of Ananias and Sapphira, which appears in Acts 4:32–5:11. It's a troubling, frightening story in which two people commit "one little sin" and God kills them. Their offense is this little, innocent thing. They lie about how much money they're putting in the offering plate. Surely in the age of grace, such a small transgression could be forgiven. Why would God kill them in that moment?

Some say that God didn't actively kill Ananias and Sapphira, but rather they were so distressed by the fact that Peter was on to them that they died of natural causes. (The text doesn't directly say, "God killed them," so it's a fair theory.) Others say that God killed them as an example, to let the community of faith know that God is holy (or some other lesson). Some commentators throw up their hands and say, "This is a difficult and frightening story," and leave it at that.

Part of our problem in understanding this story comes from a cultural blind spot. We don't see Ananias and Sapphira's sin as a big deal because it's one we've allowed to grow and become a central part of our Christian culture. That is a potentially infuriating and upsetting suggestion, but give me to the end of the chapter to make my case.

Some people start looking at this story in Acts 5:1, but it really starts in 4:32. Here we learn that the believers were "one in heart and mind" and that they gave their possessions willingly to one another. There weren't any poor people among them, because if someone was in need, someone else would sell a piece of land and there would be plenty for everyone. This was not expected of anyone. It doesn't appear that anyone passed the plate, or started a capital campaign, or gave a sermon about giving. In fact, Acts 4:33 says that this was happening because "God's grace" was "powerfully at work in them all."

That's an important point. The beautiful community in which none is impoverished and all are cared for came about not because of church governance, not because people obeyed the concepts of Scripture, not because of shared values or compassion or peer pressure but because God's grace was at work among them. These believers saw this exceptional generosity as an outpouring of God's grace. This will matter as we explore the precise nature of Ananias and Sapphira's sin.

Peter doesn't leave a lot of room for us to wonder what exactly these two did wrong. He says that Ananias lied to the Holy Spirit (5:3) and that they both conspired to test the Holy Spirit (5:9).

It seems unlikely that Ananias and Sapphira actually thought of their action as lying to the Holy Spirit. I don't imagine them in bed one night talking about their day and saying, "You know what? I bet we can trick God if we do everything just right." No doubt they realized they were lying. But they must have thought they were lying to Peter and the Twelve and the community of faith. Peter's point here, I think, is that they thought they could get away with it. They honestly believed they could lie about their gift and there would be no negative effect, no ramifications, no consequences. Their thinking revealed a radically undeveloped idea of who God is, as they soon discovered.

Why would they do this? It seems clear that they wanted to receive greater status in the community of faith by claiming accolades and praise for something they didn't actually do. They could have given half the money to the community, and that would have still been evidence of God's grace at work. Giving everything was not expected. Instead, they gave a portion of the money and lied about it, intending to take the praise for having given all.

The sin was not only that they lied but also that they lied with the intention of receiving status in the community. They represented themselves spiritually as people other than who they actually were. They figured they could pull it off, too, which revealed their small picture of the reality of God.

This was a big deal. God's grace in the lives of people was creating limitless generosity. Their lie presented a corrupted version of God's grace in the community, and they did this for their own gain. They were focused on themselves, on their status, and not on the needs of others. They were selfish. Arrogant. Prideful.

God permanently removed them from the assembly. Peter doesn't seem upset by this. He, too, saw their lie as a huge issue. Notice that the response of the community is fear but that no one asks, "What happened here? Why did God do that?" They seemed to understand.

A Cultural Blind Spot?

We find it difficult to wrap our minds around the idea that God would kill them over this, even if he was doing it as an example, or to keep the church pure, or out of righteous indignation. We find this difficult to accept because the American church is full of this particular sin. It's part of our culture. It's accepted. We wink at it. We even encourage it at times. We don't see it as a big deal because we engage in it every week.

I imagine that seems harsh. You might be wondering, *When do we in the church tell lies for the purpose of status or to represent ourselves as something different from what we are spiritually?*

Let's start with our pastors.

We have an expectation that our pastors should be able to do everything. Preach on the weekend, lead us in prayer in the middle of the week, visit the sick in the hospital, write well enough to publish a few books, balance the budget, lead the staff. They need to have the ethical skills to answer any moral question. They should be able to do premarital counseling and speak at funerals. We need them to "grow the church." We want them to be exemplary spouses and parents and to do so while spending every weekend and most weeknights at the church instead of at home.

Do we understand how rare it is for someone to be graced by God to be a good speaker, writer, organizational leader, parent, spouse, shepherd, and trainer? Those people exist, but they are few and far between.

We celebrate those who do all these things well, creating a culture in which status is determined by one's ability to "win at everything." This pressure to achieve and be a "good pastor" leads some pastors to live a double life. They can't share their sins and troubles with just anyone, so they try to find people outside the church to share their lives with. Or they cut themselves off completely. More than one pastor has told me it is inappropriate for them to have friendships in the church. Why? Because if their church members knew who they really are, they wouldn't be able to lead them well.

So pastors who are not particularly good Bible researchers start getting their sermons from the internet but present them as their own work. Pastors who can't write hire ghost writers to take their sermons and put them in book form. (Sometimes the ghost writers get their names on the cover and sometimes they don't.) Or they just straight-out steal material for their books. Several pastors have told me that there's no such thing as plagiarism when sharing spiritual things because "we all just want people to hear the gospel," so it's OK to use someone else's material without giving them credit. Pastors train their kids not to act like regular, fallible human beings while on the church property, because they don't want anyone to think the pastor isn't a perfect parent. Some pastors lie about who they are so they can have spiritual status in the church. We, the nonpastors, have built a culture that both demands this and rewards it.

It's not just the pastors. I am a missionary, in the professional sense. I have worked for a Christian nonprofit organization for over fifteen years. I grew up in the church and attended Christian schools through high school. I love the nonprofit organization I work for, I love the church, and I love many of the Christian institutions we have put in place, including Christian schools.

But let me give you, as exhibit A, my prayer newsletter as a missionary. As a missionary, my salary is paid by the generosity of those who choose to donate some of their own money to God and our mission. It's God's grace to me, my family, and my ministry, very much like in the early church. People who care for my family or believe in our ministry (or both) donate their own money as an act of praise to God, allowing my family to live and minister freely.

This is a beautiful thing. In return, I send prayer newsletters and updates to my supporters—whitewashed, positive letters about the amazing things God has done. Don't mistake me. These are true things, not exaggerated things. But do I write about our failed outreaches? Rarely. Do I talk about the hard times? Do I share my deepest concerns? Not often.

Likewise, I have to be careful in some circles not to share what television programs I enjoy, because otherwise I'll lose status in the community (because missionaries, like pastors, should be perfect) and thus lose financial support. I am leaving out the reality of who I am for the sake of spiritual status, and I'm accepting a counterfeit grace. Unlike true grace, this counterfeit grace requires me to prove my worth before I receive it.

I know missionaries who routinely lie about their ministries. They exaggerate the number of people at events, or the number of hours they work, or the number of people who have prayed to accept Christ. They do this so they will be seen as better members in the community of Christ. They are lying for the sake of their spiritual status.

It's not just the professionals.

Sometimes we get dressed for church out of respect for God, and sometimes we do it for the sake of how others in the community see us. This goes both ways, incidentally. I've been to a church where you are judged for not wearing a suit and to a church where you are judged for not having tattoos and a hip flask. We change our behaviors to show the rest of the church that we have it together, that we're in the right place spiritually.

Families bicker and argue in the car on the way to services and then sit quietly and content during the sermon, ready to fight again when they get off the church property. People are shocked and offended to hear a curse word on Sunday morning and go home to watch *Game of Thrones* on Sunday night.

We join the worship team so people will hear our beautiful singing voices.

We lead the missions team so we get a chance up front on stage.

We put a card with prayer requests in the offering plate and pretend it's a twenty-dollar bill.

We lie about who we are so that people will think more highly of us. Not just us individually but us as a community.

The thing is, it often works. The world might see us as hypocrites, but that's only because they see us as we really are. In church, we can all put on the masks and say our lines and enjoy the sound of one another clapping for the performance.

How do we break out of this cycle? How do we get out without falling down dead? I'm not sure. I'm trying to be more honest about who I am. I don't exaggerate what God has done in my ministry. I am embracing my weaknesses: I'm a good writer and speaker but a terrible, horrible administrator. I don't like doing daily devotionals, and I'm frankly not sure they're expected of us. I rarely like praise and worship music. Sometimes I like it too much when people applaud after my talk, so I've started clapping when the audience does. It's my private way of redirecting that praise to God, even though it makes me look like an insane person who applauds at the end of his own talks. I tell other ministers to take vacations. I tell them they don't have to be perfect. I try not to make decisions based on how much money someone donates to our ministry or to the church. I share my imperfections and try to love and support the imperfect people around me.

Do you know what Ananias's name means? It means "God is merciful." That might seem ironic given how Ananias's story played out, but I know that it is true. I know because I have been guilty of the sin of Ananias and Sapphira a thousand times. Our churches are soaked in it.

But God continues to show us mercy and grace.

5

The Outlaws

Drew keeps throwing a ball against the wall over and over. It makes it hard to sleep, but Bart still snores, loudly, from his lower bunk. The Twelve are all here, spread out over three cells. James and John were put in separate cells, and they talked most of the night, except when a guard came through occasionally and told them to shut up. Every once in a while Matt sings in a low voice, "Nobody knows the trouble I've seen." It drives Drew crazy, which only seems to encourage Matt. They are all nervous, scared, and bored.

Gray light filters in through the barred windows.

"Someone's coming," Thom says, nudging Bart in the ribs.

"I'm awake," Bart mumbles.

A man in white clothing walks up. A nurse?

The doors to all three cells open. "Come with me," the man says.

They all jump to their feet. Drew has the ball with him, but James grabs it as they reach the end of the hallway and throws it back into one of the cells, where it bounces crazily between the bunks. Drew looks back at the cell, but he isn't going back in there.

The man leads them out of the prison and into the public square. The crowds have just begun to trickle in. "Go tell them," the man in white says. "Tell them all about this new life."

That's what they do, one-on-one, in small groups, and as the morning goes on, eventually taking turns talking to large crowds. People shout questions, encouragement, skeptical comments.

Bart, the only one who has gotten much sleep, is the first to see the guards wandering around the square, aimless and lost. "Hey! They're looking for us."

When the guards turn toward the Twelve, the crowd surges between them. The guards try to make their way forward, but the crowd pushes back, shouting and threatening the officers. Someone picks up a stone and wings it over the officers' heads. The captain pulls his men back a few yards, straightens his hat, and brushes the dirt off his shoulders, drawing attention to the yellow badges on his sleeves.

"They're not doing anything wrong," someone shouts.

"We want to hear them!"

The captain raises his hands over his head, asking for silence. When the crowd quiets, he says, "We do not intend to harm these men. May I approach them, please? I would like to ask them a question."

The crowd parts, murmuring. Several people have stones in their hands now. The captain steps into the narrow opening and walks quickly to the Twelve. He clears his throat and says, "Gentlemen. I see that you chose not to remain in the accommodations I provided. I'd like you to speak to the authorities about this matter. If it pleases you."

Quick glances flash among the Twelve. Pete barely hesitates. "We'd be glad to join you."

The captain turns and walks them through the hostile crowd, making it clear along the way that they are his honored guests and that no harm will come to them. The crowd follows as far as they are able, until the guards fall in behind the Twelve and corral them into a high-ceilinged room. They shut the door, and the Twelve are face-to-face with the religious leaders, the most influential spiritual people in the city.

They watch the Twelve with detached disdain. At last, one of them speaks. "We ordered you not to teach about this man. Instead of obeying us you have filled the entire city with his name so that everyone is talking about him. And worse, you are telling everyone that we are responsible for his death. What do you have to say for yourselves?"

Pete speaks first, without hesitation. "You think we should obey you instead of obeying God? Never!"

Bart says, "You did kill him. You want us to keep quiet about the truth?"

Then John says, "Our God—the same God you worship, the same God my father and your father worshiped—raised Jesus, who you killed, from the dead."

Thom, full of passion, shouts, "Now God has chosen Jesus to be his right-hand man. He is our Prince! He is the one who saves us! And he will give our people the ability to turn from their evil ways and find forgiveness in his arms."

"We saw it all, you know. We were there."

"So was the Holy Spirit. He also is a witness, along with us."

"God has sent his Spirit to us, as you have seen."

"He has given his Spirit to all who obey him."

The council is furious. Various members jump to their feet, shouting back at the Twelve. "Are you saying we're not obedient?"

"So you continue to accuse us of murder!"

"Blasphemy!"

"We should kill all twelve of you, you disobedient troublemakers!"

The shouting goes on like this, both groups yelling at each other for a few minutes. Finally, one of the respected seminary professors in the room, a wise and well-known teacher, stands and raises his hands, shouting over and over for quiet. When the council continues to shout, he calls the guards over and tells them to take the Twelve outside for a moment.

The guards herd the twelve men out into the hallway. They pull the door shut behind them, and the professor nods, satisfied.

The furious council members and leaders huff, and tuck in their shirts, and sit back down, waiting for their flushed faces to cool off. They drink water and calm themselves. The teacher, Professor Gamaliel, takes the floor.

"Gentlemen, listen to me. Be calm. Think this through." He paces the floor, his hands behind his back. He is an old man, and his long white hair follows him like a comet's tail. His beard is cropped close, and his eyes are bright and shine like wet stones. "So they claim their teacher is sent from God. They claim he's the Savior. Remember that man a few years ago who said the same thing? He had hundreds of followers. And what happened when he was killed?" Professor Gamaliel raises his eyebrows. No one answers him. His eyebrows go higher, inviting an answer. Still no one speaks, so he says, "Nothing. That's what happened. His followers slunk back into their holes, and no one's heard of them since."

"They're disrupting everything!" someone says.

Professor Gamaliel laughs. "Remember that militia group a few years ago, with that man who led them all with machine guns into an antigovernment revolt? That was disrupting. I remember the news channels covering it around the clock. How did that end? It ended with the army breaking into their compound and killing the leader. Where are his followers now? Scattered like a pile of stones flung about by a small boy. Who knows where they are? Who knows what has become of them? They never mention that man or his cult on the news anymore, do they?" He answers his own question. "No. They do not."

"Their teacher is already dead, though, and still they gather followers!"

The professor nods. "Indeed. But for what purpose? Listen to my advice, brothers, and consider this carefully. If their purpose is one invented by humans, it will fail just as all the others have failed. If they truly are representing God—" He raises his hands over the objections of the council. "Let me finish. If they truly are representing God, you will find yourselves fighting against God. Is that what you want?"

"Of course not," someone says.

"Of course not," the professor echoes. "So leave these men alone. Let them go and don't think of them anymore."

The discussion goes on a few minutes longer, but it is more a matter of how to follow the professor's advice than whether to do so. Everyone agrees he has made a compelling argument.

They call the men back in. The Twelve stand in a group, with the guards all around them. One of the council members says, "We are going to let you go. But not without punishment."

The guards step toward the center, and the Twelve involuntarily move toward one another. Several guards have loosened their billy clubs from their belts. They close in on the Twelve, swinging their clubs, and the sound of hardened wood on too-soft flesh echoes in the chamber.

"That's enough," one of the council members says after a minute. He looks down on the bruised and bloodied men. A few of them are standing, helping the others to their feet. "Think about that," he says, "the next time you feel the urge to tell someone about your Jesus."

They do. They think about it and laugh, happy to have been singled out as followers of Jesus. They don't stop either. In the public spaces, in their homes, in their neighbors' homes, they never stop telling people about the Prince, their Savior, Jesus.

Wanted: Dead or Alive

One time I was in a closed country in Asia. A "closed country" is a place where, one way or another, the good news about Jesus is illegal. It might be illegal to be a Christian or, as in the country I was in, it might be legal to be a Christian as long as you keep it to yourself. But if you talk to someone about it, if you try to share the good news, that is illegal. No sharing! Or else.

On this particular day, I had made my way into a student dorm at the university, and I sat in a cement dorm room with six students. All of them knew one another, but this was the first time I had met them. We talked about all the normal things: What is your major? Do you know [insert famous American]? Why did you come to our country?

After a while, the conversation turned to family and eventually to faith. Each of the six young men in the room told me that he had no faith at all. It wasn't allowed. Some of them were passionate about this, and others were indifferent or even conflicted. One of them said, "Since you are from America, you are a Christian."

Ignoring the fact that there are many Americans who are not Christian (just as there are many in their country who are not atheist), I admitted that I was indeed a follower of Jesus. "Have you ever met a Christian before?" I asked.

One student had a relative who was a Christian . . . his aunt, I think. Most of them had never met a Christian. I was the first they had seen. I asked them if they wanted to know what a Christian believes, and they said they did.

I began, just like the Twelve, to tell them what I had seen, heard, and experienced with Jesus. I told them how he came to earth as a human being, lived a perfect life, and was killed by human beings. I told them how he came back to life on the third day and now offers a relationship with God to anyone who wants it. I asked them what they thought about that. The room was silent.

Finally, one of the students looked up at me, frowning, and said, "It's illegal for you to tell us these things."

He was right. It was illegal, and I was well aware of the fact. I could be deported or (less likely) put in jail. Either way, if these students called the police, I would end up in the back of a police car and headed to the station. Best-case scenario.

There was nothing I could do to argue against it either. I had, after all, broken the law of the land. The government would be completely within its rights to enforce that law and punish me. Which was, of course, precisely the situation in which the Twelve found themselves in Acts 5:12–42. Already, James and John had been brought before the religious ruling council for preaching about Jesus and had been told to keep their mouths shut. This ruling council, the Sanhedrin, was made up of the wisest, most experienced teachers in the country, and the Roman government had given them authority to deal with all religious matters among their people. It was well within their rights, given them by the state, to command the Twelve to stop preaching and to go back to being well-behaved religious men who showed up for church on Saturday and said their prayers and lived quiet, happy lives.

What are we to do in a situation like this?

There are those today who would say, "If a government doesn't give missionary visas, we should not send missionaries to that place." Or, "If it's illegal to share the good news in a country, we should not share there."

This comes from a well-meaning, even noble understanding of Scripture. For instance, Romans 13:1–2 says:

> Let everyone be subject to the governing authorities, for there is no authority except that which God has established. The authorities

that exist have been established by God. Consequently, whoever rebels against the authority is rebelling against what God has instituted, and those who do so will bring judgment on themselves.

That's pretty clear. Obey the government and those in authority over you because God has put them in place. It is, by the way, one of the reasons we speak with respect about our president and other leaders even when they belong to a different political party. Right?

But the Twelve, when told by their ruling authorities to cease speaking about Jesus, said, "We must obey God rather than human beings." In other words, the authority of God is higher than the authority of human beings.

God was clear that they were to tell others this story and to speak often about Jesus to all people. In the final verses of Matthew 28, Jesus said to them, "All authority in heaven and on earth has been given to me. Therefore go and make disciples of all nations, baptizing them in the name of the Father and of the Son and of the Holy Spirit, and teaching them to obey everything I have commanded you. And surely I am with you always, to the very end of the age" (vv. 18–20). Jesus said he has "all authority," and *therefore, because of this, for this reason,* they were to go to all nations with his message and teach them to follow. His authority is higher than the authority of the human governments (authority that he gave them anyway). If Jesus has all authority and commands us to go, then on this topic our authority trumps that of the secular government. There is literally nowhere on earth that is outside our authority to go and share the good news. If we allow a government to declare their country off-limits, we are putting their authority over Christ's.

So when Jesus's followers got to "closed countries" and the leaders there said, "You may enter but not tell people about Jesus," they entered and spoke the truth about Jesus regardless.

Notice, by the way, that Jesus did not promise there won't be consequences when we allow his authority to trump that of the secular government. Even in this story, the Twelve were beaten before they were released (Acts 5:40), and as time went on, many of them would be killed. Some were even executed by the government.

Lying for Jesus?

Since so much of this book is about the Holy Spirit and how he has chosen to make the good news about Jesus available to the world, and in light of the previous chapter, which dealt with lying to the Holy Spirit, I'm going to address a common objection that doesn't come up in this particular story in Acts.

I've heard people say, "If you go to a country that doesn't allow missionary visas and you intend to do missions work, then you are lying by getting a work visa, or a tourist visa, or a humanitarian visa. You cannot go to that country without lying, so you can't go there."

I don't want to write an ethics chapter here, but it would be instructive for us to take just a moment to consider the problem of bribery and then come back to the question of "lying for Jesus."

Most people agree that bribery is wrong. You can get thrown in jail for bribing a police officer or a judge in the United States, for instance. But there is a difference between offering a bribe to convince someone to do something they should not (bribing a police officer to harass your political opponent) and bribing someone to do their job. For instance, I've had border guards tell my friends they won't be allowed to enter a country despite having all the right paperwork unless they pay an extra "fee" to the officer. In the first case, the person offering a bribe is acting in an unjust way. In the second situation, the person is being forced into a bribe in order to get someone to do their job. The bribe in the first situation is designed to elicit an unjust end. The bribe in the second situation is a symptom of abuse: the person offering the bribe is being wronged.

In the situation where an entire country is marked off-limits for the good news, we must see the law as unjust. Why should some countries not have access to the good news about Jesus, which he intended for the whole world? So the question becomes, "What is our responsibility in regard to an unjust law?" Martin Luther King Jr. and many others would say that an unjust law must be broken. But does an unjust law make lying acceptable? Or perhaps a better question is whether this is a lie at all.

The early church sometimes acted in ways that skirted this line. The first-century church, for instance, began to meet in the catacombs, a series of underground tombs. Did persecuted people tell others why they were descending into the catacombs? Did they say, "We're headed down to sing praises to Jesus"? It's unlikely. Part of why it was safe was that there was a good reason for people to go into the catacombs: ancestor veneration. No one really questioned people going down there, and it was private.

Consider a similar situation today in a closed country. If a group of believers is going to meet to praise Jesus in an apartment complex, but they will all be killed or thrown in jail for it, is it OK for them to tell the apartment guard that they are having a birthday party for a friend if it's actually someone's birthday and they buy a cake? Or would that be lying?

Imagine you are entering a closed country to tell others about Jesus and you get a tourist visa, which allows you to enter the country and see the sights. Would it be lying to do that if you actually went to see the sights in addition to your missionary work?

What if you went in on a student visa and spent twenty hours a week in class learning the local language?

What if you got a work visa and entered the country as a computer programmer (or whatever work you do professionally)?

Why would writing "missionary" on your visa application be more honest than writing "computer programmer," "student," or "tourist"?

Someone might say your "real job" is a missionary. Isn't that true of all of us? When someone asks you what your job is at the neighborhood barbecue, do you say, "To tell everyone on earth the good news about Jesus," or do you say, "I'm a high school teacher"?

Ah, but it's a question of primary intent, you say. I might be a computer programmer invited to do some work in North Korea. But what I really want to do is tell people the good news. I should share my primary intent, not "lie" about my purpose in entering the country.

OK.

Once there was a guy named Samuel. He was a prophet. His king was a man named Saul, and God had decided to remove him as king. Saul was not a kind or forgiving man. One day, God came to the prophet Samuel and told him to go to the house of a man named Jesse and to choose one of Jesse's sons to be king (1 Sam. 16:1).

Samuel knew that if he followed God's command, Saul would kill him. He'd ask where Samuel was going, and when Samuel said, "To pick out the new king," Saul would kill him without hesitation. So Samuel asked God, "What should I say to Saul when he asks me where I'm going?"

God told him to take a heifer and sacrifice it and to invite Jesse and his sons to the sacrifice. "If King Saul asks where you're going," God said, "tell him you're going to make a sacrifice to me. When Jesse's sons show up, you can choose the new king." But wait. Samuel's *primary intent* was to choose the new king (King David, by the way), not to make a sacrifice. Wasn't Samuel lying when he told Saul that he was going to Bethlehem in order to sacrifice a heifer?

If that was lying, then God encouraged it in this example. So does that mean Samuel wasn't lying? Or that there was a greater moral principle at work? Either way, this story shows that God didn't have a problem with what Samuel did. In fact, it was his idea.

I'm not suggesting, by the way, that we need to tell lies to get people to believe in Jesus. In fact, I believe God makes it clear that his spokespeople should be scrupulous about being honest. It's difficult enough to believe the enormous claims of God in the good news story. A dishonest messenger would only confuse things.

I do think, though, that if lives are at risk or people don't have access to the good news, it's perfectly acceptable to answer a question like, "Are you a Christian?" with "Most Americans claim to be Christians." Or even to answer, "What is your definition of a Christian?" I don't think avoiding the question is the same as lying about the answer.

Which is why I ended up in a dorm in Asia being told by one of the students that the good news I had just shared with them was illegal. "You could be thrown in jail," he said.

I sat back in my chair and looked at the students, all six of them watching me carefully, waiting to hear what I would say. I grinned at them. "It's true," I said. "Everything I just shared with you was illegal for me to say. So I'd appreciate you not telling the cops."

Somehow, that broke the tension. I'm certain the Holy Spirit had something to do with it. In that moment, in this story, I didn't receive the consequences of breaking the law. In fact, the students all began to laugh and clap me on the back and say, "No, no, you are our friend. We would never tell the police about this!"

"Great," I said. "Thank you."

One of the students put his hand on my shoulder. "OK. Now tell us more about this Jesus." And that's what I did, despite all the laws telling me otherwise. And those six young men sat and listened, asking questions and learning about the great God we serve, despite the wishes of their government. The Holy Spirit goes where he wishes. He is not a respecter of borders.

6

Waiters and Parking Lot Attendants

Theo,

Everyone loved Esteban. He had curly black hair and a lopsided smile, and he always hurried ahead to open doors, always seemed to be the one hovering nearby when your arms were full. He was the man who took your burdens, the guy who seemed to make life easier, the whole time thanking you for letting him spend time with you.

He was one of seven men chosen by the community to help keep things running smoothly. They were named Esteban, Felipe, Enrique, Jose, Timoteo, Roberto, and Guillermo. They were waiters and parking lot attendants. They changed diapers and set up folding chairs. They made sure everyone got their fair share of food. People in the community called them the waiters. The servers. The ministers.

The entire community loved those seven, but especially Esteban. Outside the community was a different story.

Esteban was young and funny, quick with a joke. He danced when he talked, and he could win a crowd to his side with a wink and a few words. Not only that, but he spoke with power. Like the Twelve, he would preach and God would do impossible things through him. People from outside the community would line up to debate him, and he would defeat them with the good-natured and pleasant ease of an adult wrestling toddlers and then, laughing, invite them to wrestle again.

People tried to praise him for it, but he always shrugged it off and said the words came from the Spirit. "You wouldn't praise a car for flying if a tornado picked it up, would you?" Then he would grab the hands of the children and spin them around and shout, "Let's fly!"

There is a certain kind of person, Theo, who cannot stand to be beaten. If they lose an argument, they don't reevaluate their position. They don't think of new arguments. They head out to the parking lot and slash your tires. You've seen them on the internet, no doubt. The people who don't engage with the ideas of those they disagree with but attack them personally instead, making up stories, lying about their arguments, searching for false accusations to make.

Some of those who had lost debates to Esteban were of this kind. Instead of listening to him or coming back for another round, they began to lie about him. They claimed he was a heretic. They said he didn't believe in the true God. They said he had told disrespectful lies about a famous man of God from our past: Moses, God's spokesperson. They said he had threatened to blow up their house of worship.

These were serious charges, and Esteban was brought before the gatekeepers, the most influential spiritual leaders in the city, famous pastors and theologians. They listened to the accusations, which were many, and all of the leaders looked at Esteban.

Esteban did not seem troubled. His eyes were bright, his lips turned up in a small smile. No doubt he loved the idea that he had been brought before such influential people and that he would have a chance to speak to them.

Esteban's face! It's hard to describe. It wasn't like on day fifty, when flames burned over the heads of many. It was like that of Moses when he had stood in the presence of God and his face shone like chrome in the sun. It was like that of the Teacher, who lit up like an incandescent bulb about to burst. It was as if everyone was standing outside on a cloudy day, but the sun had burst through, illuminating his face. It was as if he and he alone stood in the presence of God.

Then they asked him a simple question: "Are these terrible things true?" His face! How could they even ask with that bright face reflecting God's glory?

So Esteban began his speech. He started by addressing them politely and with respect. "My brothers. My fathers."

Then he started a winding history, theological and national, of his people. He started with Abraham but spent a long time on Moses, who they had accused him of discounting.

When he began to talk about the house of God, the place Esteban had supposedly threatened to destroy, he began to speak with great passion. He practically shouted the very words God had spoken on the day his house had been built: "Heaven is my throne, and the earth is my ottoman. You think you can build me a house? Where do you think I live? Didn't I make every stone you used to build and every thread of every curtain you have woven? Didn't every tree you've cut into planks come from me?"

Overcome with emotion, Esteban turned to the crowd and shouted, "You stubborn people! You do all the rituals to appear right with God, but your heart isn't in it. Every time the Holy Spirit tries to talk to you, you fight him."

The crowd didn't like this. They started to shout back at him, to deny what he said.

Esteban shook his head and said, "You're stuck in that same old pattern, just like your parents and grandparents and great-grandparents. If God sends someone along to tell you something, you make life hard for them. In fact, you kill them. You killed the ones who promised you the coming of the Righteous One. And when he came, you betrayed and murdered him. You're so worried that I might say the wrong thing about God's Word, but you don't even do what it says."

The response from the crowd could best be described by referring to wild animals. They raged and growled and surged toward the platform. They gnashed their teeth. Their hands curled into fists. Someone jumped up on the stage.

Esteban didn't seem concerned. I've spoken to multiple people about this. He wasn't terrified or angry or begging them to calm down. He looked out over their heads, like he had been distracted. He saw something above them, beyond them. He looked through them like he was looking through glass. His face relaxed into a smile, and one hand pointed up toward the sky while the other touched his lips. "Look!" he said, and he almost laughed. "I can see straight into heaven, and the Son of Man, Jesus, is sitting in the place of honor next to God."

Then the crowd couldn't contain themselves. They rushed the stage. I don't know who punched him first. Someone grabbed him by the coat and dragged him down the stairs. They shoved him into a car, banging his head against the roof. Some of our people followed them as they drove out of town. They called the police. There were sirens in the distance.

It was clear this wouldn't be just a beating. Men were shedding their jackets, rolling up their sleeves. A young man named Saul gathered their coats to make sure their wallets didn't fall out, that they didn't get dirt or spittle or blood on their clothes. The crowd picked up bricks and bashed Esteban with them. They grabbed him by the hair and kicked him. They punched and bashed and beat him, and when he finally crumpled to his knees, he shouted, "Dear God, do not hold this against them!" As they rained down their final blows, they did so to the sound of him begging the commander of heaven's armies to forgive them for his murder.

Esteban, the waiter, the server, the gentle minister who spun children in circles, who handed out food to the poor, who set up folding chairs and always had a kind word for everyone, lay in the dust, caked in his own blood, flies landing on his unflinching face.

When the crowd was gone, when it was safe, our people covered him with an old sheet and snuck his battered body into the backseat of a car. When they got him back to the attic . . . you've never heard such wailing.

Growing Pains

From second to fourth grade, I attended a small Baptist church in Nashua, Missouri. I don't know how many people attended for sure, even though there was a wooden attendance plaque in the front with numbers that could be slid in and out to show the small weekly fluctuations. I'd guess maybe the same number that Scripture says gathered in the upper room waiting for the Holy Spirit: 120.

I have fond memories of the church. Sunday school class was in the basement, which was cool in the summer and warm enough in winter. The church had a gravel lot and just beyond that a dirt baseball diamond for the church league. It had a modest parsonage and a tall white steeple with a cross set against blue sky and enough pews to give 120 people space to set their Bibles down but still feel that the church was comfortably full.

What would we have done if three thousand people had showed up for worship? Where would they have sat? Forget sitting, where would they have *stood*? I guess we could have moved the service outside, but I don't know where we would have parked all the cars.

In one day, the early church went from 120 people to three thousand plus. From that moment, we're told, it "continued to grow." Take a minute and imagine your church or a church you've attended. How many people show up for one service? Now multiply that number by twenty-five. What sort of problems would your new, larger congregation run into?

That's precisely what happens in Acts 6.

It's no wonder the apostles needed help running things. Overnight they had gone from a large home group to a megachurch. Not only that, but their teacher and leader was gone. Plus Judas, who had always been the most organizationally minded of them, had betrayed them and then killed himself. They had gone from a scant hundred people hiding out in a wealthy friend's upper room to several thousand people woven throughout the city.

They still had a central place of worship. The temple was a sort of nucleus to all the spinning electrons of their new world. They could still meet and worship there. But now they had inherited a staggering array of lower and middle classes, of foreigners, of beggars and homeless people.

Miraculously, everyone pitched in to take care of one another. The wealthy opened their homes, those with extra beds made them available, and eventually even the money was pooled so that everyone was well cared for.

It wasn't perfect. The Twelve were constantly in high demand, traveling from house to house or standing in the marketplace and telling people the stories, teaching people about Jesus and what he had said and done. More often than not it started with those who were already part of the community. Peter or John or Bartholomew or Thomas would stand up and start the story in the place they thought best or maybe do question and answer.

But more and more the question and answer would turn to questions of logistics. Peter would be talking about the feeding of the five thousand and someone would ask, "Where will we meet tomorrow?" "Who should I give this money to?" "A family is visiting and needs a place to stay. Who can help?" "We don't have room for all the people who are coming to hear the good news. What should we tell those we turn away?"

Perhaps most troubling was the complaint that some among them were not being fed. They were poor—most of them families who had lost husbands or fathers in some way, all of them people who spoke Greek as their first language. In other words, they were the minority among the majority culture of the Jewish believers. They were sometimes called "Hellenists" because they had adopted the language and culture of the Greeks. Today you might imagine an English-speaking church that had somehow "overlooked" feeding the Hispanic or Latina widows when handing out food. It was a clear moment of institutional racism, and it troubled the Twelve.

Was it on purpose or an accident? The Greek word used when discussing those who had been left out could be translated "overlooked," which would seem to imply a simple error. An accident. Or it could be translated "neglected." Snubbed. Ignored.

Things had gotten out of hand. The Twelve couldn't keep up with the distractions and problems and details. So they called everyone together and explained the situation. The Twelve had walked with Jesus, and they had to be the ones to tell the stories, to explain what had happened, at least at first, and there were thousands of people waiting to understand all the details. It didn't make sense for them to wait tables and portion out food and do errands when others could do those things just as well. "Choose seven people," they told the community. "Wise people, with good reputations, and filled with the Holy Spirit." This pleased everyone, and they chose seven trustworthy people. The Twelve examined them, prayed for them, and set them to work.

Looking at their names, it's interesting that all seven of those chosen appear to have been Hellenists. Greek-speaking Jews. Except for Nicolas, who had converted to Christianity and was not Jewish at all. When the majority culture in the church neglected the minority—whether on purpose or not—the apostles chose to give authority to minority members of the church to make things right.

Starving the Greeks

What exactly was happening in this situation? Clearly, the community of new believers had worked out some sort of system for taking care of the widows among them. In a culture where the major breadwinner was often the husband or father, widows could slip into poverty or worse without a champion to care for them. There were rules set in place to create justice and opportunity for them, but there was an expectation that the community of faith would step in and help care for them as well.

In any case, the new believers had a system for caring for their widows. This system could have even been set up before Jesus's death. We know that he interacted with widows occasionally. One widow had her dead son brought back to life by Jesus. He watched another give the last of her money to the temple and praised her for it. James, who knew Jesus well, said that the purest expression of the Christian religion was to care for widows and the fatherless (James 1:27).

Regardless, as the community of faith expanded, the system crumpled under the weight of the new additions. Those who had been getting food continued to do so, but these newfound believers, the "Greek widows," weren't being cared for.

It's entirely possible this happened without malice. The fact that no punishments were doled out when the issue came to light makes this likely. It makes sense that the Greeks would be last to get their food. There may have been communication issues. But there were also almost certainly political and theological issues, because the Hellenists were looked down on by the mainstream Jews. They had abandoned their culture to adopt that of the Greeks, a major betrayal to the Jewish way of thinking.

So what are we looking at here? Racism? Classism? Sexism? Could be. Whatever the cause, at the end of the day, those in the majority culture were cared for and those in the minority culture suffered.

It's surprisingly common that the minority needs go unmet in our churches. It makes sense. Those in authority try to deal with the biggest needs first. What are the biggest needs typically? The needs of the majority. If seventy people need one thing and five people need something else, you take care of the seventy first. And since those in the majority culture are also the leaders of the community (at least in this story), they're less likely to see the needs of the minority because they themselves are not experiencing those needs. And minority need not mean race or ethnicity. For the Greek widows, it was culture (Jews of Greek culture) as well as class (widows were often poor) and marital status.

Whatever the reason for the minority status, the wounds of the minority are often unseen by the majority. For instance, when it comes to marital status, imagine a church with a few unmarried forty-five-year-old women. They aren't part of the married Sunday school class. They don't get to go on the moms' retreat. They aren't divorced, so they don't go to the recovery meetings for divorced people. The singles ministry is for people thirty and under.

How do you think they feel on Mother's Day when the pastor says that being a mom is the highest calling? How do they feel when all the moms stand and someone walks down the aisles to give them roses? How do they feel when the pastor starts another summer-long series on the central importance of the family? Would it be a surprise if those few single women felt that the church had little to offer them?

This happens all the time, with many groups who are a minority being ignored either willfully or accidentally. Those who are marginalized have no voice to help make decisions about things that directly impact them.

More than once I've seen (or been a part of) people trying to right the marginalization of some group in the church by having someone from the majority "represent" the minority. In this situation, for instance, we send a male leader in the church to talk to all the single women and ask them how they are feeling and to bring a report back to the leadership. The married man in power represents the single women who are marginalized instead of letting them represent themselves.

What did the early church do? They dealt with injustice regarding the minority by putting trusted, godly members of the minority in charge. That was a bold and beautiful move.

Waiters in the Kingdom of God

The Twelve decided they couldn't neglect teaching people about Jesus in order to spend the time necessary to straighten this all out. So they asked the community to choose some people to take care of it. These seven men were examined by the Twelve and found to be "full of the Spirit and wisdom" (Acts 6:3). And what were these men tasked with? Waiting on tables (6:2).

Most people would say that these men were the first deacons. *Deacon* is a word from the Greek *diakanos*, which means "servant." There are a few people who say, "Just because they were chosen to serve doesn't mean they were servants," but I figure that's sort of like saying, "They weren't waiters just because they waited on tables." In the months and years to come, there would be both men and women deacons, and it's fascinating to watch what they did as they went out into the world.

We never actually see Stephen wait on a table in the stories to come. No doubt he did. But what he was known for were the signs and wonders he performed by the power of the Holy Spirit and his proficiency in arguing with those who opposed the community of God. Acts 6:10 says that he was so wise and full of God's Spirit that no one could stand against him in an argument. That's pretty amazing.

But things devolved pretty quickly. Embarrassed by their inability to score points against Stephen, a group of people found some liars who said Stephen was blaspheming against Moses and God. In other words, he was saying evil things about them both.

This was a big deal, of course, and he was brought in to defend himself before the religious leaders of the day. This wasn't the first time someone from the new community of faith had been brought before the religious leaders of the temple. It happened back in Acts 3 and 4, when Peter and John had been sharing the good news about Jesus and had healed a crippled man. They were thrown in jail overnight until the religious leaders could convene, and when they listened to the good news about Jesus, they basically handed down this decree: Could you please stop preaching about Jesus?

That was the big punishment. For the community of faith, it was an amazing victory. Spend one night in jail and you get to tell all of the most influential leaders in the temple the story of Jesus. In return, you get a stern lecture. Peter and John thanked them for the lecture, said, "We're still going to be honest about our experience," and went home and had a big party with all the believers. This was probably how some of the Jewish priests ended up joining the community of faith.

Now Stephen was in front of many of those same leaders, and he was facing some trumped-up charges. But Stephen was so good in an argument and so universally beloved that no one thought anything bad would happen. Worst-case scenario—and this would be a terrible, worst case—he was going to get kicked out of the temple grounds and be told he wasn't welcome there. Excommunication. But it wasn't like the religious leaders had the authority to do much more than that. The Romans were in charge of capital punishment and execution. Even when the apostles were called in again after they refused to follow the instructions to keep quiet about Jesus, the high priest had them beaten and released. Surely that's the worst that would happen to Stephen.

One more thing to know. When Stephen was accused of blaspheming God, they were attacking his theology. They were saying that Stephen had a disrespectful, evil, wrong picture of God and was convincing others of it. When they said he was blaspheming Moses, they were not talking about Moses himself. It was common at that time (and still today) to refer to the law itself as "Moses." They were talking about the law, which was given through Moses. They were talking about the holy books. They were talking about the Bible. Here's the accusation: this heretic does not look at God the right way or show proper respect to the Scriptures. In fact, look at the exact words of their accusation: "This fellow never stops speaking against this holy place and against the law. For we have heard him say that this Jesus of Nazareth will destroy this place and change the customs Moses handed down to us" (Acts 6:13–14). Jesus will come and destroy the temple and *change the customs*. Stephen was preaching (they said) that God will come and do away with their religious systems and rituals and traditions.

Stephen's accusers were gatekeepers. They had created a subgroup in the religious system, and their job was to keep the religion pure. Their role was to protect the religion. They had drawn a circle in the sand, and they patrolled the edges, making sure that everyone knew who was in and who was out. They were saying, "This man can't be from God because he's saying things differently than we say them. He doesn't realize the centrality of the temple. He doesn't understand the perfection present in our traditions."

The high priest looked at Stephen, whose face was shining like that of an angel, and asked the only question he could: "Are these accusations true?"

In answer, Stephen began to tell a story, a good story about good news. He began when God appeared to Abraham, before the temple and before the law. Then he told the story of Jacob, who served God before the temple existed and before the law was spoken. Then Joseph, who followed God and saved God's people, without the temple and in ignorance of the law. Then he lovingly retold the story of Moses, who met God in a foreign land, without a temple and before being given the law.

He explained how the ancestors of his accusers and judges did not listen to or obey Moses when he spoke the living words of God, the law, the directives of the Holy One himself.

Then he told of the tabernacle, a sort of tent that worked as a mobile temple, and how that had to be good enough until the time of Solomon, and how even when his great temple was complete, God said that he would not live in a house made by human hands, because the whole earth is little more than a place to prop up his feet.

At that moment, it was clear that Stephen massively respected both Moses and God. He turned to his accusers and called them stubborn people with uncircumcised hearts. He said that every time God's spokespeople came to them throughout history, they fought them instead of welcoming them. Being circumcised was to follow God's commands, so when he said that their hearts were uncircumcised, he was saying that they might follow God's rules outwardly but that their hearts were not in the right place. They had lost the plot. They had focused so much on the rules and the regulations and the theologies that they had forgotten who provided the rules, and who was the object of those theological studies. Basically, this was the moment when the waiter comes to the table and is told he has delivered soup with a fly in it. The waiter looks in the bowl and says, "Oh. Did you want that camel in there too?"

Stephen didn't preach against the temple. But what if he did? Does the temple matter that much? God doesn't live in the temple. All the great heroes of our faith didn't have access to the temple, including Moses. Who cares if you have a temple if you aren't following God? Who cares if you have the right rituals and traditions if you perform them without thinking of the God you are supposedly serving?

Gospel-Centered, Bible-Centered Bad Guys

Of course, Stephen's accusers were the bad guys. We know this because they're about to kill Stephen, the hero. But before we get to that, let's take a moment and reflect on ourselves.

Are we Bible-centered?

Are we centered on the gospel?

Are we known for our excellent theology?

If so, we are in mortal danger of being the bad guys in this story. We are gatekeepers, drawing a line in the sand to make sure everyone knows who is in and who is out. I am going to explain this carefully, and I hope you can hear it. Please don't gnash your teeth or throw rocks just yet.

The Bible is precisely as important, beautiful, God-given, God-breathed, inspired, and useful as the law itself. The law, of course, is part of the Bible. But should I center my life on the Bible or on the Righteous One who gave us the Bible? In our history, are there those who followed God well without the Bible? Stephen named a few: Abraham, Jacob, Joseph. All of those listed in the "hall of faith" in Hebrews 11 followed God well without the benefit of the Bible that you might find sitting beside a hotel bed. Some of them had pieces of it; some had none. Some of them helped write it. None of them had what you and I have, the Bible in its complete form. They did not center their lives on the Bible. They centered their lives on the God they followed.

Likewise, for those of us who speak of being gospel-centered, we have marked out a center target that is not the bull's-eye. The good news about Jesus is undoubtedly the most important communication from God to humanity, but it is not the center of the Christ follower's life. Christ himself is the center. It's the difference between enjoying talking to your lover on the phone and being in love with your phone. We should not center ourselves on the good news but on the one the good news reveals.

We can say "gospel-centered" or "Bible-centered" and *mean* "Christ-centered," but then it's easy to drift, slowly and imperceptibly, toward being someone who worships the good news or worships the Bible instead of worshiping the Creator. The temple was massively important in the history of God's interaction with people. But it was not central.

Stephen ended his reprimand when heaven opened and he saw the one who was his center, Jesus, standing at God's right hand.

The gatekeepers were so furious that they stopped listening, literally putting their hands over their ears. They rushed Stephen and knocked him down, chasing him out of the temple and then outside the gates of the city, where they murdered him. Murdered. This is the correct word. What they did was illegal. They did not have the legal right to perform capital punishment. Even if they did, the trial was not over. No one had pronounced a death sentence.

The outsider had to be silenced. No more warnings. No more lectures. No more arguments or conversations. Only bricks held in white-knuckled hands, falling with terrible speed, targeting the skull of their opponent.

They threw punches and kicked him, and he stumbled along, praying. "Lord Jesus, receive my spirit. I'm coming home." When they knocked him to his knees, he knew it was over. He cried out, "Oh, God, forgive them. They don't know what they're doing." The poor, stubborn people. Their hearts aren't open. Of course they can't understand. Of course they don't see. Don't hold this against them.

And he closed his eyes and slept.

Outside the Circle

Usually, when someone was beaten to death for heresy, their body was left to rot. Their bones would be scattered outside the gates of the city, food for the wild animals. Not Stephen. He wasn't killed for heresy. So godly men, followers of Jesus, came and took his body and brought him home for a proper burial. In fact, Acts 8:2 tells us that godly men buried him and "mourned deeply" for him. They made a big deal out of his death, a public statement that his death had been unjust.

It was clear now. They had all thought that maybe there was a way to coexist in the temple. They were Jews themselves, after all, and Jesus was the promised Savior. They believed in God, respected Moses and the law. But it wasn't safe. A crowd had beaten one of their most respected leaders to death for what? For sharing his beliefs in a respectful, wise, careful way.

They began to pack their things and leave the city. Not everyone. But bit by bit, facing new problems and new trouble, a family here and a household there began to leave Jerusalem. They scattered like bones. They drifted away like scraps of paper in the wind. No, not like bones. Not like scraps of paper. They scattered like airborne seeds, small black packages of life held aloft by the wind and seeking a square of freshly tilled soil. And they found it wherever they landed. The community continued to grow.

Stephen was a waiter. A servant. A deacon. A parking lot attendant. No one could stand against him because the Holy Spirit spoke through him. He was the first to follow fully in the steps of Jesus, all the way to his murder outside the city. His final words revealed the character of a Christ-centered man. Stephen had become like Jesus.

Even the parking lot attendants in the kingdom of God are people to be reckoned with. You're not an apostle, not one of the Twelve, not a leader in the church . . . so what? The Holy Spirit can speak through you just as powerfully as that waiter, that parking lot attendant, that Spirit-filled man named Stephen.

7

The Effeminate Foreigner

Felipe wears tan slacks and a collared shirt, but his fingernails are always broken, cracked, and caked with dirt. He's a gentle man and quick to smile. His wife died in childbirth when their fourth daughter was born, and I detect a hint of sadness in his eyes when he introduces them to me. They are fierce, beautiful women with bright, intelligent eyes, and I'm told they speak freely in the community and are sought out as people of truth. Felipe's pride emanates from him like a warm halo. He invites me to sit in a small sunroom, and when he gives me a cracked teacup full of strong coffee, I feel the calluses on his hands. The faded china must remind him of his wife. He often traces the faint remnants of flowers on the cup in his hands as we talk. I sit patiently, blowing on the hot drink, waiting for him to begin. One of his daughters looks in on us, and he waves her away, laughing at her concern. I set my recorder on the small table between us. The red light winks on, and he takes a long breath.

"God told me to go south," he says. He mentions a road and asks if I know it.

"The desert highway," I say.

He nods. "There was a limousine there, driving across that empty road. An entourage was with it—police motorcycles and black SUVs. On the front of the limo, small flags snapped in the wind. Red, white, and black, with a green triangle."

"Why were they driving way out there?"

Felipe leans back, his eyes rolling to the ceiling as if to say, *Only God knows.* "God said to me, 'Run up alongside that limousine.'" This is the way Felipe talks. As if God doles out directions all the time. Go here. Do this. Say that. I imagine him on the desert highway, a younger man, running up to the limo of an influential government official.

"You had a car?" I ask.

He shakes his head. "I jumped a divider and ran alongside the car. As you might think, they traveled much faster than I."

"Were you afraid?"

Felipe laughs, slapping the arms of his chair. "Of course. The police had guns. I was running on the highway." He takes a sip of his coffee and watches me with a small grin on his face. "They pulled over, and one of the police told me to move along. But I had seen the government man through the window. He was reading the Bible on his tablet. So I shouted to him, 'Do you understand what you are reading?'

"His window rolled down, and he said, 'How can I understand when no one will explain it to me?' I did not understand what he meant at first. I asked for permission to come closer.

"A police officer frisked me, patted me down. He didn't find anything on me, but the officer stared at me with a cold, hard glare. The limo driver opened the door for me. I slipped inside, thankful for the cool gush of air as I entered."

Felipe describes the government official carefully. A tall man. Although, looking closer, Felipe could not tell for certain that it was a man rather than a woman. He had the darkest skin of any man Felipe had met before or since and a round but attractive face. His hair was cut nearly to the skin, and despite the air-conditioning, a slight sheen of sweat stood out on his scalp. When they shook hands, his skin was soft, even feminine. He wore a light perfume, and his perfectly tailored suit fit his thin frame like it had been painted on him. His fingers were long. "Like those of a pianist," Felipe says.

"What did he mean?" I ask. "That no one would explain the Bible to him?"

Felipe sighs. He looks down at my recorder, as if debating whether to speak. His eyes harden, and he says, "He was black. He was a foreigner. He was effeminate. He was not going to marry and have children."

I don't look away from him. "Did those things bother you?"

Felipe's eyes flicker. He turns toward the heart of the house where his daughters move about, spinning and turning in the complicated dance of a loving household. "He was reading from the book of Isaiah." He closes his eyes, his lips turning up at the edges as he quotes the ancient words. "He was led like a sheep to the slaughter, and as a lamb before its shearer is silent, so he did not open his mouth. In his humiliation he was deprived of justice. Who can speak of his descendants? For his life was taken from the earth."[1]

"What did you say to him?"

Felipe opens his eyes. "He spoke first. He asked me, 'Who is Isaiah speaking about? Himself or someone else?'"

"What did you tell him?"

"Beginning with that passage, I told him the good news about Jesus, the Savior."

His daughters come into the room now, carrying plates of food. "La comida," the first says, and her sisters are close behind. They crowd around the little table, and the six of us bow our heads while Felipe speaks a long, wandering prayer about sheep and sorrow and being washed clean and about one who carries our grief and pain. He is thankful for the hot food, and the nearness of his daughters, and the clean sunlight, and for me and my questions and a chance to tell his story once again. We say our amens and pass the tortillas around the table.

"Do you know the passage?" he asks me.

My mouth is full, but I nod.

He passes the rice across the table. "Every word of it speaks of our Teacher. 'He had no beauty or majesty to attract us to him, nothing in his appearance that we should desire him.' He was 'a man of suffering and familiar with pain.'"[2]

I try to picture Felipe there, sitting in the limo, watching the tall, thin, effeminate man in his perfectly tailored suit. He is leaning close to the man, pointing out words on the screen, swiping to the next screen, scrolling to other passages, telling this man his own story too. "Were you uncomfortable?" I ask, wondering again whether it bothered him to be with a foreigner, a black man, an effeminate single man with no plans of marrying, all alone in the back of a limousine on a deserted road.

Felipe wipes his mouth and sets his napkin on the tabletop. He reaches across the table and takes my hand. "Dr. Lucas," he says, "did you know the Teacher?"

I never met him face-to-face, which, as you know, Theo, is why I am doing this project. I tell Felipe so. I believe in him. I love him. But I have never seen him.

Felipe nods, as if this reveals something, as if my question finally makes sense. He squeezes my hand. "The Teacher was a foreigner to me." He indicates the small feast perched on the table between us. "We are not of the same culture. The Teacher did not marry. He had no children. When I looked in the eyes of that man on the desert road, I saw my beloved friend, our dear Savior, reflected back at me."

Felipe's hand burns where it touches my own. "So you weren't uncomfortable?" I ask.

"Not at all, Dr. Lucas. I was profoundly grateful to be near him." Felipe removes his hand from mine and traces the flower on his teacup. "The government man also thought I should be uncomfortable. Even after I explained the good news, he asked me, 'What prevents me? What is it about me that makes me unworthy of this good news?'"

"What did you tell him?"

"Nothing." He laughs as if this is the punch line to some wonderful joke. "I told him that if he believed, then nothing prevented him."

I sit back in my seat. Felipe wanders off from that story and is telling one now about a cult leader or magician. He is sharing stories of miracles and healings and speeches he has given here in this country, so different from his home. He spins the story of the good news as we eat. His daughters interject here and there, enlivening the discussion, correcting their father or one another. Sometimes they laugh at my questions. There is one question I ask that they must hear often, because one of Felipe's daughters answers, dropping her voice an octave to imitate her father. The sisters all laugh riotously at this.

I try to laugh along, but I am thinking of that tall, thin man. I am wondering if I would feel uncomfortable in the back of a car with him. Or in the same room. Or if he wandered into the back pew of my church. I am wondering what I would have said if that strange man had asked me what prevented him from entering into the kingdom of God. I am not sure of the answer.

A Private Audience with an Effeminate Man

Philip was another waiter / deacon / parking lot attendant put into place by the Twelve. After Stephen's death, everyone was in danger. Most of the believers left Jerusalem and scattered to neighboring cities and countries. Philip headed north, for Samaria. Once he got there, much like Stephen, he began to preach and perform miracles, healings, and exorcisms (Acts 8). The result was that the Samaritans were filled with "great joy." They were happy to have the guy there.

He had a variety of adventures, and Peter and John came to visit when they heard about everything happening. They had a small run-in with a powerful pagan magician who wanted to pay them so he could receive the Holy Spirit and then charge other people to receive it. Basically, the guy wanted to become the worst kind of televangelist and was willing to pay for a crash course, and they sent him along with a healthy lecture.

Sometime after this, Philip got a communication from God. An angel told him to go to a certain road south of Jerusalem, and to go right away. He did so and found an Ethiopian eunuch from the court of Queen Candace. Candace was not the queen's name, actually, but her title—from *Kandake*, the term for the rulers of the kingdom of Kush at this time.[3]

A lot of information is thrown out in a short amount of time. Philip saw that the man was a eunuch, he learned he served in the court of Candace, he was on his way home from Jerusalem. The man had his own scroll, which meant he was probably wealthy. He had gone to Jerusalem to worship, and he was reading aloud from Isaiah.

A few things to know about eunuchs. At this time, it was common in some countries to have eunuchs serve the royal class. Israel did not practice this. Most likely, this eunuch was born a slave. Around his tenth birthday, well before he entered puberty, he was castrated. In theory, this provided a servant who was focused on the royalty, not on children or wives or in-laws or family.

The physical effects of castration prepuberty were many, and picking a eunuch out of a crowd would be easy. Without testosterone, a eunuch would have little or no facial hair, softer skin, would likely be taller, and would never have to worry about male pattern baldness. His voice would not have dropped, and, obviously, he could not have children. He would generally be seen as more effeminate than a typical man.

On the religious side, things might have been frustrating. Acts says that he had gone to Jerusalem to worship, but a eunuch was not welcome in the temple. Deuteronomy 23:1 says, "No one who has been emasculated by crushing or cutting may enter the assembly of the LORD." For someone who had not been born a Jew, there were two categories of participation in Jewish religion. A person could be circumcised and agree to follow the entirety of the law and be allowed into the temple, including into the inner courts of the temple. This was off-limits to the eunuch because he was "emasculated" and because he could not be circumcised. It's possible that he could be a "God-fearer," which meant that he could not enter the inner courts but he could be a part of the external worship at the temple.[4] Nonetheless, the eunuch had multiple things that prevented him from entering fully into worship at the temple: he was a foreigner, and he was physically imperfect.

When Philip asked the eunuch if he understood what he was reading, he replied, "How can I . . . unless someone explains it to me?" (Acts 8:31). I like the way the New English Translation expresses it: "How in the world can I, unless someone guides me?"

But the eunuch had just come from Jerusalem, where all the greatest minds in Judaism lived. He had, at some point, paid someone to copy at least the scroll of Isaiah for him. Even now, headed home, he was reading it aloud to himself. Surely someone could have explained things to him while he was in Jerusalem.

Perhaps the damaged foreigner wasn't worth the time for the religious people. And in his case, there were literal gatekeepers preventing him from entering the community of God. When he asked, "How can I, unless someone guides me?" it may have been much more than momentary frustration.

Philip, instructed by the Holy Spirit, climbed into the chariot with the man and, beginning with Isaiah 53—a stunningly beautiful chapter focused on describing the coming of the Savior—told the eunuch the good news of Jesus.

It's easy to imagine how Philip shared the good news of Jesus with this man when looking at Isaiah 53. He started by talking about the ugly one, rejected and despised by human beings, the outsider, the outcast, the man who knew what it meant to suffer. Philip started by telling the eunuch about the man who knew what it was like to have people turn their faces away when they saw him, embarrassed.

Then he started into the metaphor. Jesus took our pain for us. He took our suffering, sins, iniquities, transgressions. He took the punishment for those things. We were like sheep who kept wandering off from the flock. He took the punishment that brought us peace. He died and then saw the light of life.

All of this Philip connected to the story of Jesus, who walked among the people of Israel and taught them. He showed them miracles. He healed them. Then he was crushed, pierced, bruised, murdered. Three days later, he stood and walked out of his grave and offered a life like his to any who would follow.

What Prevents Me from Being Baptized?

Who knows how long they spoke and what other things Philip explained? We do know that he at least taught the man about baptism. In Jewish culture at this time, baptism was a ritual that was widely understood. It was a symbolic act to remove sin and evil from one's life. The idea was that sin and evil made you "unclean." In baptism (a Greek word that means "immersed" or "dunked"), you agreed that your sin was evil and that you would no longer embrace it in your life. Then you washed yourself clean in living water. (Living water meant running water.)

Baptism in the first century was done naked. Some churches today (like Orthodox churches) continue this tradition. The early church practiced this as well, and an early source, Hippolytus, tells us, "[The baptismal candidates] shall take off all their clothes. The children shall be baptized first. . . . After this, the men will be baptized. Finally, the women, after they have unbound their hair, and removed their jewelry. No one shall take any foreign object with themselves down into the water."[5] In fact, it's likely that one of the important reasons to have female deacons was that they performed the women's baptisms.

St. Chrysostom said that people went into the water "as naked as Adam in paradise," and St. Ambrose said that people went naked into the water just as they came naked into the world.[6] Not only were clothes removed but so were other foreign objects: rings, bracelets, hair ties. Baptism was a ritual of rebirth. You came out of the water reborn. The high points of baptism were these: the rejection of sin in your life, entry into the living water that cleanses, entry into new life reborn.

As the chariot continued on its journey, the man saw some water nearby and asked this question: "What prevents me from being baptized?" No doubt he meant this literally. Which of my defects prevents me from entering into this new life and the community of Christ followers?

My nationality?

My castration?

The fact that I will never marry?

The fact that I will never have children?

Philip's answer: none of those things. If you believe the good news about Jesus, you can enter the water.

The man did believe, and they walked to the water's edge. The eunuch removed all of his clothes. It's beautiful to me that the defect that kept him from the temple was now on full display as he entered the community of Christ followers. The eunuch revealed all of his flaws, all of his insecurities, and let them be washed away in the living water. Then he went away rejoicing as Philip disappeared.

The Holy Spirit saw a man who thought he could not enter fully into the community of faith, although he desperately wanted to do so. The Spirit spoke to Philip and sent him on a journey to find the man where he was, alone in the desert, and to bring him to the community of faith, to life, to the living water. That's beautiful.

I wonder who is alone and wandering the desert, seeking home, unsure if they can approach God and our community? I wonder who has been told by the gatekeepers, "You can come no farther toward God"? I wonder who the Holy Spirit has chosen for us to seek out and share the good news about Jesus with?

A Great Honor

Felipe has come back to the story. The meal is long since over, the dishes cleared. "Nothing prevents you," Felipe says. "There are so many who will give you a list, an encyclopedia of barriers between you and God. But nothing prevents you as long as you believe."

"What did he do? What did he say when you told him that he could follow Jesus?"

Felipe smiles. "The man ordered his driver to pull the limo over near a stream of water. I waded into the water. The shock of the cold took my breath away. I called for the man to join me. The police stood nearby, arms folded. The limo driver stood near the limo, his shiny black cap in his hand."

"And the man?"

"He stood at the water's edge. He stared at the sunlight on the rippled surface for a long time, and then he shrugged out of his jacket. He placed it on the ground, then his tie, his carefully pressed shirt, his undershirt. He took off his shoes and tucked his socks inside. He expertly folded his slacks and placed them on the shirt."

"Did he take off . . . everything?"

"His scars, Dr. Lucas. You are a doctor. You have seen such scars before?"

I nod. More than once.

"They shone like the stars in the universe, Doctor. Every place where he was broken. Every scar, every wound, every evil thing that had been done to him and by him and for him and through him. They shone brighter than the chrome on the car, brighter than the reflections on the water, brighter than the sun itself. I knew such things could no longer keep him from the Holy One. I called out to him, 'Do you turn your back on all the wrongs in your life, all the sins and evils you've committed?'"

"What did he say?"

"He ran into the water. He shouted over and over, 'I do, I do, I do!' We went down into the water, and he came up whole, newly born, newly alive, newly a son of God."

Felipe turns his head from me, and I see him wipe at his eye with a knuckle. "The Spirit whisked me away," he says. "The last thing I saw was the water sparkling as it flew from his laughing face, his hands thrown up in the air as he danced from the water." He wipes his eyes again. "It was a great honor, Dr. Lucas, to have been his guide. It was a great honor to make the introductions between that beautiful man and the Lord Jesus."

8

Those Who Are Far Off

I am walking down Straight Street with Ananias. He has crooked, yellow teeth, which he is quick to show when something amuses him, and he walks with his head bowed as if in prayer, his hands folded behind his back. Cars barrel past on the wide road. He stops outside a gated fence, his wrinkled hands firm on the iron bars. Beyond it there are oak trees and a grand house peeking out above them. He flashes his uneven teeth at me. "This is the place."

I move for a better view. The house is three stories, wide and with wings. It's early evening now, and warm lights are just coming on in the many windows. Someone stirs in the guard's station at the far end of the gate. Ananias motions for me to follow, and we walk past the guard, dipping our heads toward him and then following the sidewalk alongside the fence until it transforms into a long beige wall, its upper edge a few feet above us.

"What was it like in those days?" I ask.

"Terror, Doctor. Refugees poured in, hiding in our homes. Followers of the Way were afraid to speak freely because of what had happened to Esteban."

"But no one else had been killed?"

He shakes his head. "The religious leaders, though, began to use their authority to punish anyone who fell outside the circle they had drawn. They kicked them out of the community, or they imprisoned them. Sometimes they were beaten when they were held for trial. Most had fled the city, though, and thought they were safe."

We wait for our light at an intersection. "But they weren't satisfied to let the people run?"

"No, because our people, wherever they went, would not stop talking about Jesus. They kept telling the story, and like any good story, it was contagious. The story grew. One person heard it on the street, and, astonished, she shared it over dinner with her parents. Her father, confused and disbelieving, shared it with his priest. The priest, uncertain what to think and concerned about losing power, shared it with his superiors. It moved into homes through tiny cracks, like a mist. It burst out of any prison cell, strong as a lion. It couldn't be contained or controlled, only heard or received or retold."

I am looking at Ananias's face and the fierce pride in his eyes. A sedan honks at a semi as it makes a right-hand turn, and I realize our light has changed. I motion to Ananias, and we cross the street, then meander into the city park. We make our way down a path as the first streetlights flicker on, the bugs beginning to gather in their glow. We sit on a park bench, the peeled green paint giving way to smooth wood, and we enjoy the warm night air. I take out my notebook and recorder. Ananias nods, and I touch the tip of my pen to my lips for a moment. "They tried to destroy it though? Didn't they?"

Ananias sighs. "Of course people tried to destroy it. They tried to stamp it out like fire. They beat it with branches. They blew on it, they fanned it, they threw water on it. But the water only caused it to spread. Trying to restrain it was like trying to grab hold of the wind. Trying to stop it was like trying to put smoke back into a fire. Yes, the story burned, and every person it touched was irrevocably changed."

"Like Saul," I say.

"You should have *him* tell you the story," he says.

"I will." I had already heard it more than once. "But *your* story . . . he doesn't tell it well."

Ananias's eyes crinkle in amusement. "No, he does not tell other people's stories well, does he?"

"Do any of us?"

"For me it started with rumors. Rumors of a devout, religious young man. Serious. Passionate." He puts a hand over his mouth, then rubs his hand down over his chin. "They say he had a briefcase full of handcuffs and zip ties. He would break into homes where Jesus followers lived. He and his friends would wrestle them to the ground, handcuff them, pack them into a minivan, and ship them off to trial."

"Everyone was afraid of him."

"Only those who believed Jesus was sent from God feared Saul. The conservatives held him up as a champion. When they heard young Saul and his men were coming, it was as if electricity had been shot through the religious community. Some found it dangerous, even deadly. Others were energized by the potential of his presence."

A couple walks past us pushing a baby stroller. They are young and in love, and look exhausted. The baby sleeps peacefully. I look at my notes. "But on his way here, Saul met Jesus on the road."

Ananias nods. "He had a vision and was blinded. Again, he should tell the story."

"Of course, of course."

"I also had a vision. In my vision, I was on my knees praying in a dark room. I felt someone enter behind me and place his hands upon my head, and I knew it was the Lord Jesus. I turned to look, and he smiled at me. He said my name, and I said, 'Here I am, sir.'"

"What did he tell you?"

"That I should go to the very house we just walked past and find this Saul. He would be expecting me. I would find him praying that he would no longer be blind."

"Were you frightened?"

Ananias laughs. "I am not a young man, but I am not foolish either. I told the Lord Jesus, 'I have heard that this man has caused much suffering among your followers, and even now he has come to this city with the authority to imprison your people.'"

I write these words down, surprised that this gentle old man would speak back to the Lord himself. "But you went."

"Yes. He said, 'Go! I have chosen to use this man for my own purposes. He will speak my name before politicians and foreigners and his own people. He has caused others to suffer because they called on my name. I will show him how much he must suffer for the sake of my name.'"

"I'm surprised they let you in the house."

"Saul had been told I was coming. He had left word with the security guards to let me through. I went up the stairs to his guest room. He was on the floor. He had not bathed in days. His hair was unkempt, his face contorted, his voice hoarse. I suppose he had been praying and crying out for days."

This must have been quite a blow to those who had been waiting for Saul, the avenging angel of theology, to sweep into town and imprison all who had opposed them. Instead, they had this blinded, weeping wreck of a child curled in the fetal position on the floor, refusing food and mumbling ceaseless prayers.

"I bowed down over him and said, 'Brother Saul, the Lord Jesus—the same person you saw on the highway—has sent me so that you can see. He has sent me so that you can be filled with his Holy Breath, the Spirit.'

"As I said those words, scaly flesh fell from Saul's face. He blinked, then covered his eyes with his arm. He lowered it slowly, blinking in the sudden light, and he took hold of my leg, weeping again. He had done terrible things, he said. He caught sight of his briefcase full of handcuffs and leapt to his feet. He slammed open the window and threw the briefcase out, the handcuffs sailing into the air like shining coins, then bouncing through the lawn.

"He turned to me, tears still making their journey down his face. He wanted to be baptized. Immediately. He stood and disrobed, making his way to the bathtub, and I dunked him there, in the presence of the house staff. Someone brought him some food, which he ate gratefully while toweling his hair dry.

"After he had eaten, his host came into the room and asked if it was true, that he had become one of the followers of Jesus. Saul said it was true, indeed. His host told him that, regretfully, he was no longer welcome in the house. Saul took his bags and left the house without looking back."

Enemies of the Good News

I spent a few hours on Facebook tonight looking at who Christians list as enemies of the good news or of Jesus. The president of the United States was listed. Various legislators were mentioned, and at least one Supreme Court justice. Some radical Muslims in other countries. Gay people. People who hate gay people. Atheists. Hollywood as a sort of monolithic entity was listed, mostly because of a handful of popular television shows. Progressive Christians. Conservative Christians. And so on.

If I think back to my own childhood, I can come up with a spectacular list of things well-meaning believers told me were from the pit of hell and thus at war with God (and I am not exaggerating): Dungeons and Dragons (demonic). *Star Wars* (New Age propaganda). Teletubbies (gay propaganda). Rock and roll music. Smoking. Wearing sneakers to church. Reading a Bible that wasn't the King James Version. The pope. A woman showing her navel in public. Anyone who encouraged anything on the aforementioned list.

I don't list these things to make Christians sound ridiculous (and maybe you agree that some of the things on the list are evil—I don't know). I do believe that there are people out there who see themselves as enemies of Jesus and who specifically target Christians or the Christian faith to antagonize, persecute, and attempt to destroy it. I put that list together as a sort of starter for this question: Who would you put on the list of God's enemies? Or at least Christendom's enemies?

Certainly, there are people who are God's enemies. Saul himself (who later calls himself Paul) says in Romans 5:10 that we were once "God's enemies." It shouldn't be a surprise that Jesus has enemies. If there were people in opposition to Jesus when he walked around in Jerusalem, why not after his death and resurrection?

Who Are the Bad Guys?

Confession time. I am a father, and I dearly love my three daughters, but I don't always make the best decisions. I try, but sometimes I mess up. A good example is that I once allowed my four-year-old to watch me play a Cold War shoot-'em-up video game on our TV. It didn't scar her or make her violent. It did make her decide that she loves "the gun game," and she asks me to play it all the time. I don't do it often, because I have mixed feelings about her watching it. One day I did let her watch me play, as I guided my British spy hero through a series of Russian military installations. She leaned up against my back, put her head on my shoulder, and said, "You think they're the bad guys. But they think *you're* the bad guy."

I was stunned by her insight. She probably could have cleaned up the Cold War in a couple of weeks.

A natural human impulse is to create "good guys" and "bad guys." We want the hero to wear a white hat and the villain to wear a black hat. We like the conflict to be clear and morally unambiguous. To the infant Christian community in Acts 9, Saul has placed the black hat firmly on his head.

The Christians wanted to worship in peace. They had respectfully shared their views in Jerusalem, which had gotten some of them beaten and one of them killed. Not wanting to further endanger themselves or cause trouble in the religious community, they had scattered to other cities, where they could worship in peace. Saul, not satisfied with that, had gotten permission to hunt them down, trap them, and drag them back to be tried, found guilty, and thrown in prison. He was a terrifying villain.

From his point of view, he was a defender of the faith. He was passionate about the Scriptures, dedicated to the faith, and a serious student of the law. He didn't want false doctrines spreading. He didn't want a cult sneaking its way into good people's lives. Allowing a cult to escape to other cities wasn't acceptable, nor was the cultists' desire to be left alone. They may have wanted to be left alone, but they kept telling people that Jesus was the Promised One from God. To the conservative Jewish community, Saul was a rock star, a hero, an example to hold up to your children, someone to be emulated not feared.

Ananias, on the other hand, as a follower of the Way, found the instructions from God troubling. Wasn't it a good thing that God had blinded one of their persecutors on the road? Wasn't it good that he was hiding out, sobbing and praying in a guest bedroom of some rich person's house? When Ananias got his marching orders ("Go find Saul and pray for him so that he can be healed"), he actually talked back to God.

It was like this.

God: Go to the house I'll show you and pray for Saul that he can see again. I've already told him you're coming.

Ananias: Yeah, but . . . God, I realize you're all-knowing and everything, but just a reminder that this is the guy who has been throwing all of your people in jail. He's caused a lot of trouble.

God: Do what I say because I chose this guy to take my good news to all sorts of people, including pagans and kings and the people of Israel. And I'll show him how much he will suffer because of my name.

Ananias: You got it, boss.

What was Ananias thinking on the way to the house of Judas, where Saul was staying? Me personally, I would have had some questions. Why can't God use one of the people already following him instead of Saul, for instance? Would it be that big of a deal to ask *me* to talk to the Gentiles, kings, and the people of Israel? Why does it have to be Saul? And what if I heal Saul and the guy goes crazy and starts arresting people anyway? What if his encounter with Jesus on the road hasn't created lasting change? What if, in other words, I am giving help to the enemy?

To Ananias's credit, if he had any of those questions, he didn't reveal a bias when he got to Saul. In fact, he even called him "Brother Saul" when he arrived. He prayed for Saul, and when Saul could see again and had eaten some food, Ananias immediately baptized him. Notice that Ananias didn't just pray for Saul's sight to be restored. He prayed that he would "be filled with the Holy Spirit" (Acts 9:17).

It's an interesting story. In fact, it's surprisingly similar to the story of the Ethiopian eunuch. Someone in the faith community had a vision to go find an unlikely person. When they did so, they performed a service that opened someone's eyes, and then that unlikely person was baptized. We'll see this again in the next chapter. It's no coincidence that Luke strung these stories together in this way.

Far Away from God

For me, one of the most compelling observations about the story is this: those who are farthest from God can become great assets to the work of the good news. Don't write people off. Don't dismiss them because of their hatred of God or God's people. Don't ignore them because of their devout devotion to another religion. We are not able to judge someone's spiritual readiness to become a follower of Jesus.

I'll share this example from my own life. A friend took me out to do some "random evangelism." To be honest, I'm not a huge fan of this. Going up to a complete stranger and trying to start a conversation about Jesus can be terrifying. It's like running up alongside a chariot and asking a eunuch if he understands what he's reading. My friend and I prayed together that God would lead us to the right people and that the conversations would be ones that would allow us to talk about Jesus.

We were in the Hub at the University of Washington, which is basically the student center. I just had to pick someone to talk to. You want to pick someone who wants to talk about something, anything, and will be willing to talk about spiritual things. I started looking around for someone "easy." I saw him right away. He was sitting alone, wearing headphones, studying. No one likes to study, I figured, so he would probably talk to us.

I walked over and started the conversation with a smooth introduction like, "Hey, do you want to talk about spiritual things with me?"

This guy, though, was not put off by my awkward entrance. He took off his headphones and said, "I would love that. I've been wanting to talk about spiritual things with someone." I remember thinking, *Wow. He must really need an excuse not to study*.

I pulled up a chair. I asked him some questions about his own spiritual life, and he told me he was Buddhist—not just Buddhist but a devout, deeply committed Buddhist. "My whole family is Buddhist," he said. "But even they say, 'Why do you have to be so Buddhist all the time?' I'm one of the most serious Buddhists I know."

We started talking about Buddhism and what he loved about it. It's a beautiful religion, and there are many things about it that are attractive. Honestly, though, the thought that was going through my head was that I was wasting my time. There was no way this guy wanted to hear the good news about Jesus, let alone respond to it. He was way, way far away from Jesus.

Then he said something interesting. He said, "You know, I love Buddhism, but there's one thing that bothers me."

"What's that?"

"The Buddha is not a god. The Buddha said not to worship him. But honestly, that's what many Buddhists do. We worship him. I wish there was someone who came along and said, 'I am God. You should worship me.'"

I stared at him, shocked. I wasn't sure what to say. I said something to the effect of, "Uh, I know a guy like that."

He looked at me with real interest and asked me to tell him more. So I told him the good news about Jesus, who came as a human being and lived among us so that all people can come to God. I told him the story about Jesus, born as a human baby, growing up with his family, his ministry, his sinless life, his death, his resurrection. I showed him places in the Bible where Jesus revealed himself as God, where he said that he was the way and the truth and the life, and explained how he equated himself with the great I AM.

When I was finished, I asked him what he thought.

He said, "I guess I'm a Christian now."

I want to write people off. I look at their lives and decide whether I think they're ready for Jesus. I see a militant atheist and think, "Enemy of God." I see people with deep, deep sin in their lives and think, "They're not going to give that up." I see devout people in other religions and think, "They're far from Jesus."

But this kid at the University of Washington—God had already been preparing him for the good news. He'd been revealing the good news to him through a source I found unlikely. He'd been revealing himself to this kid through the teachings of the Buddha. I came along and said a few words, and the Holy Spirit spoke to his heart and he became a follower of Jesus. This guy went from devout Buddhist to follower of Jesus over the course of a fifteen-minute conversation.

That's pretty amazing.

It's also a good reminder. Ananias was not responsible to decide if Saul was ready to become a follower of Jesus. I am not responsible to decide if people around me are ready for the good news. That's between those people and Jesus. It's my job, as God's servant, to deliver the message. How they respond is, in so many ways, not my business. Those who are farthest from God can become followers of Jesus and great assets to the good news.

This should affect the way I look at people around me. When I see an "enemy of God," I don't need to start sharpening the knives. I don't need to head to Facebook to make sure everyone knows the bad guys are coming. I'm not Paul Revere. I need to listen to the voice of the Holy Spirit and ask the question, "Could it be that God is calling this person to himself?"

A Last Thought concerning God and His Enemies

I don't want to give the impression that I have an unconcerned naïvete about the state of enemies in the Christian life. I'm not saying there's some sort of protection for all of us that means we will never come to harm as long as we follow God's will and that his enemies will always fall before us, blinded or converted. I'm suggesting, rather, that our attitude toward our enemies should be like God's attitude toward his enemies.

They may kill us, just as Jesus was killed. What did he say about them again? "Father, forgive them. They don't know what they're doing."

They may beat us to death with stones, as Stephen was beaten to death. What did he say? "Lord, do not hold this sin against them."

They may approve of the death of God's people. They may imprison or beat or terrify us, just as Saul imprisoned and beat and terrified the people of God two thousand years ago. But what did Ananias say when he saw him? "Brother Saul." Then he baptized him, welcoming him into the community of faith with open arms.

Following the Spirit's direction may lead to triumph or death. Conquering kingdoms or being torn in two. Receiving back our dead or joining them. The conversion of our enemies or persecution at their hands.

Nonetheless, as we become more like Christ, our attitude toward our enemies must be transformed. Jesus said, "Love your enemies and pray for those who persecute you" (Matt. 5:44). Some might say that God is above this, that we are meant to love our enemies but that God has a deep, impassioned hatred for those who are not his followers. I've heard this said more than once. That is not so. Jesus tells us to love our enemies in *imitation* of our Father God. To love our enemies is part of the process of becoming perfect as God is perfect (Matt. 5:43–48).

Don't forget. "While we were enemies of God, we were reconciled to him through the death of his Son" (Rom. 5:10). He died for us when we were still his enemies. God loves his enemies, and he expects us to do the same. He desires to bring them to himself and be reconciled to them. He wants them to come home. We must do away with the mind-set that those opposed to us are our enemies (even if that's what they are) and instead treat them with kindness, love, and respect. Our enemies are objects of God's love.

There is no guarantee of protection, but we need not fear the Sauls of this world. Our fight isn't with other human beings. Our quarrel isn't with flesh and blood. When Ananias started praying, he saw Saul, the enemy of God. By the time he reached Judas's house, he saw Saul, his brother. God healed Ananias of his blindness as well. God taught him to see Saul as he was: a broken man who was less powerful than God. A man in need of compassion, healing. A man who needed to be cleansed in living water.

Lord, give us the courage to approach you in prayer and speak honestly about our enemies. Open our eyes and allow us to see them as you do. Teach us to love even our enemies. Help us to follow the directions of your Holy Spirit, just as Stephen did. Just as Philip did. Just as Ananias did.

Smuggled into the Kingdom

Saul wasn't a small man. He had to tuck almost into the fetal position to fit in the trunk of the car. He had been making a lot of noise after coming to Jesus. After being baptized, he had made himself presentable and begun immediately to tell everyone that Jesus is the Way. He became worse than those he had come to arrest. His former allies were embarrassed and furious. Their rock-star example, their ideal man had turned his back on everything he had stood for and was attempting to corrupt the same religious community he had been protecting.

There were those who wanted to chain him with his own handcuffs. More than one person suggested chaining him with all of his handcuffs and throwing him off a bridge, preferably with some concrete on his feet. The police had begun door-to-door searches for Saul after the last weekend's worship service. Sirens sounded across the city as black-and-whites tried to get to the latest site where Saul had preached.

It was too much. Saul decided he needed to go see the Twelve and explain what had happened. The followers of Jesus came together and decided they would smuggle him out of the city. One of the men brought his car, and they stuffed Saul in the trunk. They piled baskets and groceries around him and threw a blanket on top in case the car was stopped.

It seemed like a strange way to sneak the man out, and I say so to Ananias. He laughs. We've talked deep into the night, and insects crowd the glow of the streetlights. Bats lunge in and out of the yellow pools of light. An occasional neighbor walking a dog wanders through the park, but mostly we're alone. I ask him what's so funny.

"The irony of it." He grins at me. "That violent, angry man who threatened us all with murder. A few days later, we are packing him into the trunk of a Ford Focus, squeezing cartons of eggs and bags of chips into the corners of the trunk, with a blanket handy to spread on top of him. To see him curled up there, his sweaty hair glued to his head . . . it makes me laugh that we were ever afraid of him."

I am writing this all down. "A Ford Focus?" I ask. "That seems small. Saul isn't a giant man, but it must have been a tight fit."

Ananias grins. "Yes, after Saul was safe, I had a word with the brother who loaned us his car. His other car was a Suburban."

"What? Why did he loan the Focus then?"

Ananias claps me on the shoulder, and I help him to his feet. We start the walk back to his house, enjoying the warm night air. "He claimed because it got better mileage. But I have to tell you, Doctor, that I think it takes some of us longer than others to see our enemies as beloved family members."

"You think he did it on purpose?"

"Oh, I know he did. He and Saul are good friends now. Saul calls him 'Brother Ford.'"

I'm not sure I'll include that in the book, but I write it down anyway.

9

The Sail

"I couldn't pray because I was hungry," he says. He looks almost embarrassed to admit it, the way his eyebrows raise, his eyes turn to the side, his mouth curls up in a half smile. He's one of the most respected leaders in our community, and this is how he starts his story. He stops for a moment, pulling on a rope attached to the sail of the boat we're on. "I had gone out on the upstairs porch to pray. I was having a hard time praying over my grumbling stomach, so I went back inside and asked my friend Simon to get a meal started for us."

"What time was it?"

"Around noon." He ties the rope off, then cracks the swollen knuckles of his right hand. "I've always been one to eat early. Out on the water all night, early to bed, early to eat. But that day—every time I started to pray, my stomach would make more noise than my voice. It was distracting, as you can imagine. The sun was beating down on me. I could hear Simon and his wife clanging pots around in the kitchen, and I was annoyed with them for eating so late and with myself for trying to pray instead of helping with the meal. I was frustrated at my own inability to pray."

I can't help but like him. I've heard stories about his hotheaded youth, but they are impossible to believe. He's soft-spoken and self-effacing, a straight-dealing and gentle man. I've heard this story before, but only secondhand. "It's ironic that you were so hungry given what happened next."

He rubs a hand through his thick beard. He grins. "Yes, I thought that at the time. But to be honest, I was thinking about a time earlier in my life, when the Teacher asked me to pray with him and I kept falling asleep."

"Ah yes." I grin back at him.

I told you that story in my last book, Theo, when Pete fell asleep over and over when he was supposed to be praying. At last, Jesus came to him and said, "Why are you sleeping? Get up and pray so you don't give in to temptation."

"Were you in danger of falling asleep too?"

Pete laughs now, and he's the sort of man who puts his whole self into it. It's a great, earth-shaking belly laugh that squeezes his eyes shut and forces his wide mouth open. "No! The sun was baking my poor balding head, and a fly kept landing on me, and my stomach was growling, and I was getting angry at everyone and couldn't concentrate. As I grew angrier at myself, I suddenly saw myself clearly."

I close one eye, trying to figure out that final sentence. "You mean you saw yourself clearly because you realized you were getting angry at people for things that weren't really their fault?"

"I mean that I stood up, paced around the porch, and looked back and saw myself bowed down on my knees, my weary arms propped in front of me. I saw my bald patch and the gray in my beard. I saw that accursed fly sitting on my forehead. I was outside of myself."

"You had a vision."

"More like a trance. I couldn't move my body. Then I saw it, coming in the distance, like the sail of a ship." His eyes go unfocused when he says it, as if he can see it even now. I can't help myself. I turn around and look over my shoulder, where he is staring. But I see only a white spread of clouds. "A sail let down from heaven," he says, just as I turn my attention back to his weatherworn face. "I hadn't been out on the water in a while, but I know a sail when I see it. Only this sail wasn't full of wind. As it came closer, I could see each corner was held up into the sky, and inside the sail were all manner of animals. Snakes. Crabs. Shrimp. Pigs. Centipedes. Bats. Sharks. On and on, all sorts of creeping and crawling creatures, none of them fit to eat."

I stop him there. "Forgive me, Pete, but could you explain that? I wouldn't eat a centipede, but I like shrimp. I love bacon."

Pete looks confused for a minute. "You understand all this, Dr. Lucas."

I point to my recorder and the little red light and then to the pad of paper in my lap, scrawled with a physician's scribbles. "For my audience, sir."

"Oh yes." He settles back against the boat. "Hundreds of years ago, God told my ancestors that there are certain foods that must not be eaten or used as sacrifices. Those that were acceptable to God were called 'clean,' and those that were unacceptable were called 'unclean.' Our people have built our lives around eating in the way that is acceptable to God."

"So all those animals on the sail were 'unclean'?"

"Right. It's not that they aren't edible. It's that it would be a sin to eat them, because God specifically told us, very carefully and straightforwardly, 'Do not eat those.' My father had never eaten them. My grandfather. My great-grandfather. My great-great-grandfather. For me to eat one of them would be an insult to my family, a sin against God, and the destruction of my track record of following God's commands my whole life."

"Thank you for explaining. So you were hungry, and then you saw a sail full of animals you couldn't eat. What happened next?"

"A voice spoke to me, a voice with great authority. It said, 'Peter. Stand up, kill, and eat.' I looked over the sail, hoping maybe I had missed a little sheep or a calf. Maybe a quail was hidden in among the pigs. Nothing edible was to be found. I looked it over and over, but I saw only unclean, worthless, useless animals. I said to the voice, 'Sir, I can't do that. I've never eaten anything I shouldn't—nothing unclean or unacceptable before God.'"

"How did you feel at that moment?"

"Hungry. Scared."

"Why were you scared?"

Pete sighs and looks up at the sky above us. A white cloud scuds across the blue expanse, and I think of what he said: a sail let down from heaven. "I was scared because I knew the voice. God was speaking, and here's what he was saying: 'Peter, I want you to sin.'" He scratches his beard nervously. I can see, even all these years later, it makes him uncomfortable. "I was terrified."

"You talked back to God?"

"Yes. I told him I would not sin. Not on purpose."

"What did he say?"

"He said, 'When God has cleaned something, do not call it dirty.' Then he said again, 'Peter. Stand up, kill, and eat.' Again I told him, 'Sir, I can't.' He told me not to call something unclean if God has made it clean. Then a third time the voice said, 'Peter. Stand up, kill, and eat.' I told him I couldn't, and he said, 'Do not call filthy that which God has cleansed.' The edges of the sail tucked upward, and the entire sail, animals and all, flew into the sky. I watched it rise and disappear behind the clouds, just as I had watched the Teacher rise into the sky and disappear years ago."

The lapping water against the hull fills the silence. A distant shorebird calls. The gentle rocking of the water seems to work like a massage on Peter. He closes his eyes and lets out a deep sigh. His shoulders relax, and his face loosens. "What did it mean?" I ask.

He opens one eye, his eyebrows raised. He folds his hands over his chest, closes his eyes again, and leans back against the mast. "I wondered the same thing. I found myself in the kneeling position, and I could hear a man down by the front gate of the property calling and asking if a man named Peter was staying at the house. I wiped the sweat from my face and wondered what God could be saying."

"Maybe he was telling you to abandon the dietary laws."

"I had no idea. At the time, that seemed unthinkable. But as I wondered, the Holy Spirit made it clear. He said, 'Three men are waiting for you downstairs. Don't hesitate to go with them, because I'm the one who sent them.' I stood and wiped off my knees and walked downstairs. Outside, three foreigners waited at the door. Three, just as the Holy Spirit had said, and just like the number of times God had told me to kill and eat. Three times. 'Should we let them in?' Simon whispered. 'They're foreigners. They're unclean.'"

Pete moves his shoulders. They pop, and he settles in more comfortably. His thick beard lies on his chest like a blanket. His breathing grows deep and regular, and the hairs of his mustache move with his quiet exhalations. "'They're not unclean,' I said. 'Do not call what the Lord has made unclean.' We invited them in for a meal. We ate together—finally, thanks be to God!—and in the morning, we saw wonderful things." His voice trails off, but then he says again, "Such wonderful things."

He begins to snore. I set down my recorder and notepad and watch the azure sea. The taste of salt, the cool spray, the sun baking my skin. I close my eyes and think about Peter's story. No one would begrudge him a few minutes' sleep. There is no one for miles, no way for anyone to reach us with a message, unless they unfurled a sail and dropped it from heaven. I write in my notebook until he awakes.

The Shepherd's Apprentice

Walking along on a beach, one of the last times they walked together, Jesus commanded Peter to do something. Peter took this command seriously, and it changed his life. Jesus said to him, "Feed my sheep." Within weeks, the hotheaded, self-centered Peter found himself and his peers in leadership of a burgeoning religious community. By the beginning of Acts 10, when Peter saw the sheet lowered from heaven, it had been less than ten years since Jesus had left. The selfish, hotheaded Peter had grown up, replaced by an unrecognizable sage who had earth-shattering visions before lunch and traipsed off on Spirit-fueled quests to answer the spiritual questions of strangers.

Peter had become a sought-after teacher. He traveled from city to city, telling people stories of his time with Jesus, straightening out misunderstandings, solving problems, and showing God's miraculous power. A decade ago, he had been a fisherman, but now he cast the nets for human beings. He had been beaten for the faith, questioned by the highest religious leaders in Jerusalem. He was a confident holy man, bringing wisdom and the power of God wherever he went.

We start with a story about Peter coming across a bedridden man named Aeneas. Peter walked into the room and told Aeneas, "It's time to get up. The Savior, Jesus, heals you." Then he added, "Make your bed too." Aeneas got up, and everyone was amazed.

Soon afterward, two men arrived from a nearby town and begged Peter to come with them. So he did. He arrived to find that a beloved follower of Jesus named Tabitha had died. Her friends kept showing Peter all the beautiful clothes Tabitha had made for the poor. People were weeping, telling Peter what a wonderful woman she was. Peter sent everyone out of the room and stood over Tabitha's empty shell for a moment. She had been washed and prepared for burial. He knelt down, his back to her, and he prayed. When he finished praying, he turned around and said, "Tabitha, get up." Her eyes flew open, and when she saw Peter, she sat up. He took her hand and helped her out of bed and down the stairs to see all of her friends. Of course, everyone was amazed.

It had been fewer than ten years since Jesus had left, and this was the man Peter had become. He was famous among the community. He was the sort of man you hear is a few towns over and you run to see him, hoping he can help you with your problem. Even if that problem is that a beloved friend has died.

Peter stayed with them there in Tabitha's hometown. He moved in with someone named Simon, a tanner. Now we reach Acts 10. Peter was on the roof praying and had this strange vision about "unclean" animals. He was told to eat them. This would be the equivalent of God giving you a vision in which he tells you (multiple times) to do something you know to be sinful. This isn't precisely the same thing, but imagine a sheet in front of you with needles and piles of cocaine on it and a voice that keeps saying, "Go ahead and shoot up." Peter's response was a polite version of, "Are you crazy? There's no way I'm going to do that."

I talked to a rabbi friend of mine about this. He's an orthodox rabbi in California. We talked on the phone, and I explained Peter's vision to him. He is a follower of the law, and he holds the dietary laws in high regard. I asked him, as a devout practitioner of Judaism, how he would expect a Jewish person to respond to a vision like that, where God is directing him to break the (extremely important) dietary laws. He said that he thought someone like Peter would see it as a metaphor and would ask, "What is God communicating through this metaphor?" and would be unlikely to jump directly to the conclusion, "Now I am allowed to eat a ham sandwich." Acts 10:17 seems to back this up, saying that Peter was "wondering about the meaning of the vision."

Peter didn't have to wonder what the vision meant for long anyway. The Holy Spirit explained that there were three men waiting downstairs. They were not Jews, and Jewish practice at the time was to avoid contact with those who weren't devout Jews. It was too easy for even a well-intentioned Gentile to accidentally cause a Jewish person to transgress one of the purity laws. Which meant the Gentiles were treated as unclean, just like the animals in the vision. But the Holy Spirit told Peter to go with them without hesitating.

What was the Holy Spirit up to here? He was teaching Peter a lesson. His vision was a communication designed to say, "Peter, you have some beliefs and prejudices and thoughts that make it hard for you to see what I am about to do among the nations. Set them aside so you can do what I ask of you. Don't call those whom I have created 'unclean.'"

The Holy Spirit made it clear to Peter. You are not to call other human beings unclean. There were ramifications to the vision that Peter may not have understood at that moment related to the dietary laws, but the Holy Spirit kept talking to him about *people*. God used the symbolism of the vision and the perfectly timed arrival of the messengers to tell Peter that he needed to see the Gentiles (non-Jewish people) as "clean" and acceptable to God even though everything Peter knew told him that they weren't. God trumped Peter's cultural and religious understanding with a specific communication.

Dirty

The next day Peter followed the foreign men to another city, a beautiful Roman seaport called Caesarea. There he met the Roman soldier Cornelius, who Scripture describes as both devout and a God-fearer. This means that Cornelius had refused to worship the Roman and Greek gods and had chosen to follow the Hebrew God only. He was wealthy and a commander of a significant number of soldiers. The text says he was a captain of the Italian regiment and a commander of either the entire or a portion of the cohort (a Roman cohort was as small as 480 or as large as slightly more than 1,000 soldiers).[1]

When Peter walked into Cornelius's lavish home, the soldier fell on his knees and thanked him for coming, showing something bordering on worship. Peter told him to get up. "I'm just another human being." An ordinary person just like you.

Peter was led through the house until he came to a large group of people Cornelius had invited to his house in anticipation of Peter's arrival. They were the dirty, unclean, unsanctified, imperfect people of Caesarea. They were not Jews. They were not part of the community of faith of the new Christians. Some of them may have been, like Cornelius, God-fearing foreigners. But Peter should not have been walking into this house, not if he wanted to stay clean. You can't stay clean if you wallow in the dirt.

Peter's speech in Acts 10:27–29 makes this clear. As a Jew, he was not to associate with or visit people like those gathered in this home. But, Peter said, he had a vision in which God told him that he "should not call anyone impure or unclean" (v. 28). Notice that he has already internalized the message as being about people: he shouldn't call "anyone" impure. Not "anything."

This is an important point to consider. For Peter, his vision was a communication from God with one basic point: there are not classes of human beings. There are not certain ones who should be called clean and others unclean. While Peter had believed for many years that he should not associate with the "unclean" of humanity, God told him otherwise. As a Jew, Peter would have usually refused to walk into the house of a Gentile. He would have refused to sit and eat with them or attend their parties or weddings or funerals. He would have kept himself pure by remaining separate from them.

The Holy Spirit was correcting Peter, telling him not to build a safe place away from the "dirty" world. He was telling Peter not to build a hermetically sealed religious community where he never interacts with anyone but people like himself. As we've seen already throughout Acts, God surprises the people of faith by constantly widening the circle of who is "in."

We learned in the story of the Ethiopian eunuch that there is room in the Christian community for the *believing* foreigner. We learned in the story of Saul that even God's enemies can be allowed entrance into the community. Now the Holy Spirit has said something more. It's not only the believing people who should be treated with respect but all of humanity. Peter learned that it was not his place to call any human being on earth unclean.

This insight hits me in the gut. Are there people I see as unclean? Are there people I refuse to associate with? And perhaps the most convicting way to ask this question: Are there people I see as lesser than me?

The answer must be yes. Whether I look at my own heart or at Christian culture, I see evidence of areas where we refuse to interact with others because, at the heart of it, we see ourselves as better, more clean, more correct, more holy, more spiritual, more righteous, more dedicated, more committed, more insightful, more innovative, or more traditional.

Be honest. Have you seen women treated as if they are unclean in the culture around you? I think you have. I know a single woman who was told she could never ride in the same car as her boss because it would be a "temptation." I understand this was meant as a protective measure. A protective measure for what reason, though? To keep her boss pure sexually. There is an underlying assumption that the woman is unclean and could compromise the cleanliness of her married boss.

Be honest. Have you seen people with differing theologies treated as unclean? I have. I've watched Calvinists and Wesleyans tear each other to bits in vicious online arguments. I've seen it in person too. I've seen arguments devolve into name-calling and mischaracterizations. I've seen professors asking questions about whether Genesis is literal or symbolic removed from their teaching positions, even when they can still sign off on the statement of faith of the Christian university at which they teach. Why? Because we are afraid of being "infected" by the wrong theologies.

Be honest. Have you seen people of other sexualities treated as if they are unclean? I know you have. Have you seen people of other races treated as inferior? Yes. Even in the church? Yes. Have you seen people of different political beliefs belittled? Have you seen unwed mothers treated as if they have the plague? Have you seen divorced people treated as if they have a permanent stain on their lives? Have you seen victims of sexual abuse treated as if *they* are the evil ones?

Peter did not say that all human beings have equal understanding of who God is. He did not say that all ideas about God are equally excellent or that we should accept the sinful lives of others without reservation. But he did say that God showed him that we are all made by the same God. We are made, together, in God's image. Even the sinner, the pagan, the heretic is worthy of our respect. The people of God are not better than those who do not know God. The people of God need not wall themselves off and refuse to interact with those who have lesser knowledge.

The Reason We're Here

Peter still didn't know what was going on. The poor guy was praying on the roof, was told by the Holy Spirit to go with the messengers, and heard that Cornelius was a devout man who had been told by an angel to send for Peter. Peter gave his introduction, and then he asked the inevitable question: "Why am I here?"

Cornelius told him the story: an angel said to send for you. So I did. Now tell us everything the Lord has taught you.

Peter, amazed, agreed to tell them the good news of peace, which he described as this: Jesus is Lord of all (Acts 10:36). That is the word of the evangelist, the one who brings good news.

As Peter told the story of Jesus, the Holy Spirit fell on those who were listening, and they began to speak in tongues and praise God. Peter's six companions were amazed that the Spirit had come upon these uncircumcised outsiders. Full entrance into Judaism required certain changes and the observance of the law. These people were being admitted into the community, obviously approved by God, without adherence to the law. Peter turned to them and said, "Who wants to try to prevent this? If God says they're in, who are we to say they're not?"

Peter and his companions gladly baptized the entire household. Cornelius and all his friends and family begged Peter and his friends to stay, and there is every indication that this is precisely what they did. They welcomed these new believers gladly into their community and stayed and interacted with them as if they, too, followed the law.

A quick note on the progression of Luke's argument in the book of Acts with this story. We started with the eunuch. He was a foreigner and a believer in God, but he could not make the necessary changes to become a full participant in the Jewish community. There was a vision sent to Philip, who arrived and preached the good news at the Holy Spirit's instruction. The eunuch believed and was baptized, and Philip was taken away by miraculous means. The next story, the conversion of God's enemy, Saul, has the same pieces in a different order: vision, belief, the Holy Spirit, miracle, good news, baptism. Now we have it again, this time with God-fearing Greeks who could convert fully to Judaism should they choose to do so: vision, good news, belief, the Holy Spirit, the miracle of tongues, baptism. In all three situations, God's human messengers arrive and share the good news at the prompting of the Holy Spirit. The Holy Spirit is sending his people to share the message whether the recipients of the message are enemies like Saul, or eunuchs, or foreigners.

As Peter said, "I now realize how true it is that God does not show favoritism but accepts from every nation the one who fears him and does what is right" (10:34–35). Those who could never be fully accepted as well as the enemies of God and those who hovered just outside the temple—all of the people that Jesus's followers assumed were outside the scope of the command to "go and make disciples"—are welcome in the kingdom of God if they choose to enter.

Introducing the Wind

Pete stretches his arms and makes the sounds of someone stirring to wakefulness. The sun has splashed into the water, orange and purple giving way to the coming night. Pete turns his face to the wind. "We'd best make our way home," he says, though I see him take a quick glance at the water, as if he's debating fishing for a while.

"What did the rest of the Jesus followers say," I ask, "when you got back?"

He's pulling up the sails. "All the things you would expect. Some were amazed by the story and that the Holy Spirit had been given even to the Gentiles. Others said I had dirtied myself by going into their homes and had disobeyed God by obeying God."

"Did you tell them that belief is what mattered now? That the foreigners knew and understood the good news about Jesus?"

Pete ties a rope in place and falls happily beside the rudder. "I told them it wasn't about either of those things. It wasn't about right action. It wasn't about belief."

Lights are coming on at the shore. "How can that be? I don't understand."

"Okay, I'm exaggerating. Belief matters, of course. It's essential. But for Cornelius and his family, the most significant thing that happened wasn't that they learned something new. They had heard about Jesus already, they were just missing a few key details. It wasn't that they decided to follow new laws. They had been following some of the law . . . as much as was required of them as foreigners. The thing that happened that day didn't have to do with their beliefs or their relationship to the law. The thing that changed was that they were introduced to the Holy Spirit. Certainly our message was a part of that, but we weren't amazed because they accepted the message about Jesus—we were amazed because the Holy Spirit accepted *them*!" He looks up as a seagull soars past. "Everyone praised God about that. He had given the gift of repentance that leads to salvation to even the Gentiles."

The wind picks up and fills our sail, and Pete steers us toward home.

10

Hero Worship

"Walk faster," Paul says, and I rearrange the notebooks in my arms and push farther into the crowd, trying to keep up with him. I had thought he might be a short man, but it's fair to say that Paul is unremarkable in every way: neither short nor tall, not particularly handsome nor ugly, not a flamboyant dresser. Today he wears a simple suit. It looks as if he bought it off the rack and never had it tailored. If the man wore a bow tie, he'd be the perfect picture of the rumpled professor who emerges from the research library, blinking in the light. He has thin, curly brown hair and a spotty beard. The only striking feature about him is his eyes. They are black and sharp, darting about and taking in everything. And his boxer's nose, which looks like it has been broken more than once. Like those of a boxer, his eyes do not flinch when they look at danger. He can take a punch.

Joseph, or, as everybody calls him, "Barnabas the Encourager," comes up alongside me, helping me keep my notebooks from avalanching to the ground. "You're doing well, Dr. Lucas. Paul is always running from place to place. You'll get used to it."

"Less talk, more walk," Paul says, his piercing eyes pinning us. There's an open mike event at the town square, and Paul has every intention of capitalizing on it.

"What will you do at the open mike?" I ask, increasing my pace to come alongside him.

"Tell them the good news about our Lord and Savior, of course!"

The Encourager says, "Tell him about the time they thought we were gods."

Paul sighs, pushing his way through the audience. "While I told them the good news, I noticed a man in a wheelchair. He had clearly been in it for a long time. I could see in his eyes that he believed the message, so I looked at him and told him to stand up. Which he did."

"The crowd went crazy," the Encourager says. "Absolutely crazy. They were hanging on every word Paul said after that."

Paul shakes his head. "Not really. They thought it was all coded messages meant to enforce their own beliefs."

"They had a myth in their own religion about two gods who had come to their neighborhood but no one noticed. No one would give them any hospitality. The gods later punished the entire neighborhood. This crowd was determined not to make the same mistake."

Paul snorts. "So they made a different mistake. One of their priests came, intending to burn incense to us, pray to us, give us money, and bow down to us."

There's a knot in the crowd that even Paul can't sever, so we're standing still for a minute. The Encourager says, "When we saw what they were doing, we were horrified. We ran down into the crowd to stop the priest. We were shouting and begging them not to offer such things to us."

"I snatched the incense from the priest's hand and begged them to listen to our words."

"Paul cried," the Encourager says.

Paul scowls at him. "We were both choked up."

"In fact, I'd say he wept. Sobbed. They could barely understand him he was so emotional."

"Humph," Paul says. He has found a hole in the crowd, and the microphone is in his sights. He squeezes forward, and the Encourager and I push ourselves into the momentary space of his wake. "I'm a passionate man."

"Even then, with Paul's eloquent speech, it was hard to convince them."

"What did you say, Paul?"

"I told them we were ordinary human beings just like them. I told them that the power they had seen didn't come from us but from the God who made all things. The massive expanse of the sea. The dome of heaven. The very earth on which we stood. And all the birds and beasts and sea creatures in those places. I told them we had come to bring them good news, that the God who had let them run their own way in the past had come at last to bring them home and that all along he had been reminding them of his presence. He sent them many good things. Out of his kindness he gave them rain so they could have crops and food to eat. He filled their hearts with joy."

I consider that for a moment. "What did they say to that?"

"They thought they would still give us a sacrifice, just in case," Paul says.

I laugh, but the Encourager raises a finger, warning me to stop. "They didn't like the idea that we were ordinary people. They wanted to believe we were divine."

The crowd undulates in front of us. Someone has pushed in the front. Maybe in response to Paul's shoving. "We're almost there," he says.

"So once they realized you were ordinary people, they must have all decided to follow Jesus."

The Encourager gives me a pitying look, as if he can't bring himself to tell me what a stupid statement I've just made. Paul is not so kind. "Of course not. Once they realized we were human, they hated us. It wasn't long before the crowd turned into a mob."

"How does that happen?"

The Encourager grins at me. "You might find out tonight."

"It's a short distance from adoration to abhorrence." Paul taps his fingers on his lips. "They didn't want to hear that we were ordinary. It made them feel . . ." Paul pauses, searching for the right words. It's not something I will see often. "It made them feel below average. We prayed and a lame man began to walk, a man who had lived among them their entire lives. If we were ordinary, and they couldn't do the same, they must be less than ordinary. No one wants to hear that. They wanted to destroy us out of self-preservation."

A hole opens in the crowd, and Paul shoves himself through, moving in a matter of seconds to the stage. He's at the stairs already, talking to someone with a microphone. I can see them leaning toward each other, trying to hear in the midst of the throng. I turn to the Encourager. "So what did they do? The crowd?"

"They beat him nearly to death. A few punches, then a great deal of kicking. Some bricks. Someone stomped on his hand more than once. Then they dragged him seventeen blocks and dumped him on a corner. They thought he was dead. So did we. But once the crowd dispersed, his eyes flickered open and he stood up. He walked back to our hotel. I couldn't believe it. We left the next morning." The Encourager clicks his tongue against his teeth. "I would have hated to be the maid cleaning up the hotel room the next morning. There was blood everywhere."

Paul is on the stage now. Looking more carefully, I can see Paul's fingers are crooked, barely able to wrap around the microphone. They look as if they've been badly set more than once. The man must be in perpetual pain.

Paul's voice echoes out over the crowd. "Hello, friends! I have some good news for you."

The crowd roars its approval.

Gods in Disguise

Ordinary people just like you. Paul, Peter, and the early followers of Jesus often assured people that they were everyday, ordinary human beings. Of course, they healed sicknesses. They brought the dead back to life. They preached a message of forgiveness and a return to the good graces of God. But they were just "regular people" like you and me.

The people of God are controlled and empowered by the Holy Spirit. It's the Spirit who heals and brings the dead to life. It's the Spirit who makes the connections between human beings and God. But over and over, people are confused by this. The messengers look enough like the Master that worship seems to be a correct response.

In Acts 14, the people of Lystra were waiting for God to appear. In fact, part of the reason they were so intent on making sure Paul and Barnabas knew that they'd figured out they were gods in disguise was that their region had missed the presence of the gods before.

There was a famous story about Jupiter (Zeus) and Mercury (Hermes) coming to visit not far from Lystra.[1] The gods were in disguise and tried to find a place to rest, but at a thousand houses the doors were locked. They finally found a poor married couple who invited them in and gave them a humble meal. The old couple was rewarded, but the gods said that their neighborhood would receive "just punishment for their impiety."

It's no wonder that the people would think that maybe, just maybe, Paul and Barnabas were those same gods, testing them once again. So they called Paul Hermes (the messenger, because he talked so much) and Barnabas Zeus. When Paul and Barnabas assured them that they weren't gods at all, the people were skeptical. "We just saw you heal a lame man," they said. "If that's not the work of the gods, what is?"

Paul and Barnabas denied it, of course. They strenuously denied it, tearing their clothes (a sign of deep mourning in their culture) and begging the people not to treat them as gods. In the end, Paul received a vicious beating when some of his former friends showed up and stirred up the crowd against him and Barnabas.

The human impulse to worship sometimes kicks in without us noticing. We want heroes. We want men and women who are larger than life, who we can look to with awe and reverence. We followers of Jesus may not want extra gods, but it would be nice to get some demigods. This impulse leads us to lionize athletes, politicians, and movie stars. And ministers.

It makes sense. The best of these ministers speak the words of God to us. They help us sort out our lives and deal with difficult situations. They help us move through family issues, visit us in the hospital, preside over our weddings and our funerals. Maybe they pray for us and we receive healing. Maybe they introduce us to God. Perhaps they've brought the miraculous presence of God to us in a real way. Is it any wonder that once in a while we catch ourselves offering to treat them as gods?

In chapter 4, we talked about the sin of Ananias and Sapphira, the desire to hide our spiritual realities from one another so that we can receive kudos from the community. It's a damaging sin that rots the community of faith.

This impulse to worship one another is strangely similar, only instead of lying about ourselves, we lie about those we respect. We tell ourselves that "surely a person God uses like that is special."

Not just special but chosen. Anointed. Gifted. Unique. One of a kind. Indispensable. Essential. Central to our ministry.

How many of those words are legitimately used of other human beings? How many of them should be reserved for God in the flesh, Jesus himself? Why do we create flesh-and-blood idols out of those we respect? I suspect there are two major reasons.

First, like the crowd at Lystra, we don't want to hear that these amazing people in our lives are "just like us," because if that's the case, why are we not more like them? I have a friend who is unceasingly filled with the kind compassion of God. He speaks gently to his family (even when his kids are driving him crazy) and to the people around him. Even strangers. I want so badly for him to be a superhuman. But he would say that he's an ordinary person walking in the power of the Holy Spirit. Which means, of course, that I am capable of acting with the same saintly kindness that he does. I don't want to hear that. I don't. I want to think that he has something more than I have, something that lets me off the hook for my own behavior.

Second, also like the crowd at Lystra, we have a hard time embracing the complexity of human beings. We want them to be good or evil, to wear the white hat or the black. We don't want to hear that our heroes are flawed. We don't want to know when terrible people do noble things. It blurs the lines. It makes us uncomfortable. We prefer to think that those we respect are gods in disguise.

Precious Puritans

An excellent example of this principle at work happened in 2012. A talented musician named Propaganda wrote a song sharing his thoughts about the Puritans. As an African American man, he shared a concern that certain people adore the theological insights of the Puritans (which are many) at the expense of acknowledging the sins of the Puritans (likewise many). Specifically, he addressed that the same wonderful theologians who could provide prayers like those found in the book *The Valley of Vision* were also chaplains on slave ships. They owned slaves. They beat them. They whipped them. This is historically verifiable fact.

"But wait," you say. "Not all the Puritans owned slaves." True. They didn't all have amazing spiritual insights either.

So Propaganda said it's hard for him as an African American man to listen to a sermon quoting the slave-owning Puritans, especially when that sin isn't acknowledged from the pulpit. But the thing is that we *can't* acknowledge that the Puritans were involved in heinous sin and simultaneously expect our churches to embrace their profound spiritual teachings. We can't allow our spiritual heroes to be villains. To be human. To be, in fact, people we look at in horror today: slave owners.

Predictably, a minor controversy brewed on the internet in response to Propaganda's song. There was some concern that the conversation wasn't nuanced enough. Some worried that young people might be discouraged from reading the Puritans (because the Puritans were sinners?). No one said that we should ignore the sins of the Puritans—not after Propaganda brought them up.

We have a tendency to perfect our heroes. We put them high enough on a pedestal that we can't see their flaws. We make excuses. We defend or ignore their sins. We aren't satisfied with human, flawed heroes. We want them to be perfect.

But they aren't perfect. They are broken human beings, just like you and me.

Jonathan Edwards owned slaves. John Calvin, the great theologian, agreed to the execution of a man because he didn't believe in infant baptism or the Trinity. Martin Luther, the Reformer, wrote a book called *On the Jews and Their Lies,* which is full of the worst kinds of anti-Semitism. Martin Luther King Jr., the incredible civil rights activist and preacher, failed to properly attribute a number of quotes in his doctoral dissertation. In other words, he plagiarized.[2]

Is it possible to be a person of faith, a person of influence, and have a life without controversy? Certainly it is. But not a life without sin. Not a perfect life. There are some wonderful men and women of God who aren't racist, who aren't bigots, who haven't stolen anything or lied or cheated or murdered, and yet they still aren't *God*. We must learn to embrace the fact that someone may be a gifted preacher and still be an unkind or angry person. Or be a loving person who is a terrible organizational leader. Or be a spectacular minister who is sexist.

We fail our brothers and sisters when we put them on pedestals. Instead of seeing God at work in them, we endanger them by treating them as tiny gods themselves.

It is a danger. It's a danger because if they start to believe our lies, they may cease to seek greater holiness in their own lives, deceived into thinking they are something better than all the lowly humans around them.

It is a danger because we may tempt them to claim credit for God's work or, even worse, to accept praise that should be God's alone. This can be difficult to discern. I remember catching myself thinking once, *I can't take a day off because the ministry will fall apart.* That's deadly, idolatrous thinking. God can't take care of your ministry for one day without you? Really? Are you so central to your ministry, to your church, to your nonprofit organization that God can't keep it together for twenty-four hours? Or a week while you go on vacation? Or a month while you go on sabbatical?

When I lived in Asia, our team was enormously effective. Hundreds of people prayed to receive Christ. At one point, our leadership wrote to ask us what we were doing, what was making us successful. Were we praying more? Somehow relying more on God? What were we, the human beings, doing to make our ministry successful?

We were following God and allowing him to work through us. We were listening to the Holy Spirit and trying to respond to his direction. Reading our Bibles. Praying. Following God's instructions. That's it. So were a lot of other teams, some of whom had little or no spiritual response from the people.

I remember someone asking, "Are you *sure* you're not praying more than other people?" Could it be that you're responsible for all of this and you don't realize it? No. Much to our chagrin, our prayer times fell well within the realm of "average."

Even today, as someone who has written a few books and speaks at events around the world, the temptation to buy into the lie that I am more important than other human beings presents itself. I recently spoke at a high school camp where someone said, "You're a big deal. How did this camp get you here?"

I am not a big deal. I am a human being just like you.

One time I spoke at a college student retreat in New York State. They had invited me out to talk about "The Good Life," and we were having a lot of fun. Most of the students were from New York City and had lived there their entire lives. When we told them we were having a "hayride" later in the week, they had to look it up on the internet.

At lunch one day, I took my cafeteria tray and navigated the crowd of college students before finding a table with an empty seat. I asked the students sitting there if I could join them. They looked at me with confused, strange looks and said that I could. I set my tray down, but confused by their weird looks, I asked them if they were sure it was OK. They assured me it was. I asked them their majors, how school was going, whether they were enjoying the retreat.

Finally, one of the students explained why she had reacted the way she did when I had asked to sit at their table. "My pastor would never do that," she said.

"Never do what?"

"Sit and have lunch with us."

I scratched my head. "He wouldn't? Why not?"

"He has his armor bearers."

I didn't know what that was. So I asked her to explain.

"They're his helpers. Wherever he goes, they walk on each side of him. If someone tries to come up to speak to him, they hustle him along and keep the people from talking to him."[3]

I had never heard of such a thing. "Why would he do that?"

"He's an important man. He's a man of God, and he needs to stay focused on his work, not get distracted talking to the common people."

The common people. Her pastor, too, is a common person. Just an everyday follower of Jesus. An ordinary human being just like her.

When we find ourselves the object of hero worship, it's important that we react well. Paul and Barnabas show us the correct way to respond in this story. Reaffirm your humanity. Explain the superiority and beauty of God. Prevent others from worshiping you, with tears and mourning if necessary.

There is another story in Acts of a man who tacitly accepted the adulation and worship of the crowd. In Acts 12, King Herod, the same man who had ordered the death of the apostle James (v. 2), took to a speaking platform and began a public address. As he spoke, the crowd began to shout, "The voice of a god, not of a man!"

He's perfect! Amazing! Listen to him!

Herod said nothing. He continued his speech. He did not deny being a god. He did not remind the crowd that he was a human being just like them. He did not redirect their praise to the one true God. So an angel from God struck him down, and he died.

The Jewish historian Flavius Josephus also recorded this event.[4] He tells us that Herod lived for five days, while his stomach pains wore him out on his way to death. According to Josephus, the last words of Herod were something like this: "You call me a god and now I am commanded to leave this life, while Providence shows your words to be a lie. You called me immortal and now I am being hurried away by death."

Let us accept the gifts and generosity of those who love us with humility and thankfulness, but turn away worship. Let us remind one another that we are all human beings. May God make it easy for us to say, "I am a human being just like you."

For all of us who wrestle sometimes with the desire to be great, let us be reminded of the words of the ordinary human being Martin Luther King Jr., who said, "If you want to be important—wonderful. If you want to be recognized—wonderful. If you want to be great—wonderful. But recognize that he who is greatest among you shall be your servant. That's a new definition of greatness."[5]

11

Breaking the Law

Theo,

Reproduced here, for your benefit, is a letter written by the Twelve and the leaders of the Christ followers. It was sent out at a time when there was uncertainty about what was expected for a follower of Jesus, whether they had to follow all the same rules that God had given to the Jews. I think you'll find it interesting.

Hi there.

We're told that certain messengers arrived and gave you a list of rules, telling you that you weren't following God unless you followed the rules. We didn't send those messengers, nor did we approve their message. We hear their presence and their message has distressed you and caused you to question your standing with God.

We'd like to set your minds at ease, so we're sending our dear friends Paul and the Encourager—men who have put their lives at risk for our Master, Jesus, the Savior. We're sending Judas and Silas along too, to make sure you know that this message is legitimately from us, the leadership.

We've prayed and discussed this situation, and of those laws you've heard, we and the Holy Spirit have come to agreement that you needn't be burdened with anything more than this:

- Don't eat food sacrificed to idols.
- Don't eat animals that have been strangled or that are still alive.
- Don't get involved in sexual immorality.

Avoiding these things will be to your benefit.

Sincerely,
The Twelve and the Leaders in Jerusalem

The "Seven Rules"

In Acts 15, the key question being asked yet again is this: What does it take for Jesus followers to be part of the community of faith? Paul and Barnabas, the Encourager, got in a series of arguments with other (also Jewish) believers who thought that not only should the new believers make a decision to follow Jesus, but they should also be circumcised (the sign of God's agreement with the Jewish people, marking them as his) and follow the law of Moses (a grace given to God's people).

It's important to note that members of the early church at this point still considered themselves practitioners of Judaism. They saw all the new converts as people entering the Jewish faith too. In the midst of this sharp disagreement, one thing everyone agreed on was that the elders and the Twelve were the right ones to answer the question. So a big meeting was planned, with people from both sides showing up for the conversation.

It was a question of acceptance. Should the non-Jewish believers be accepted into this "new Judaism" if they chose not to become fully Jewish? Peter stood up and reminded everyone that the Holy Spirit was a strong sign that the non-Jews were accepted by God just as readily as the Jews, despite them not being circumcised or following the law of Moses.

Paul and Barnabas were given the platform to tell the stories of what God had been doing through their ministry among the non-Jews. Everyone listened carefully. James stood up and quoted from Scripture, showing that God had always planned to take a people for himself from the Gentiles. He shared a few of the laws that he thought all believers should follow, regardless of being Gentile or Jew, and suggested that they send their decision off to all the believers. The assembly agreed on this together, and the note was sent along with Paul, Barnabas, and, to make sure everyone knew it was legit, a couple of men from the leadership team.

It appears that what James and the rest of the leadership settled on is what is called the Noahide Laws in Judaism. I'll explain briefly. After the flood, God gave some rules to Noah and his family. Since all of humanity descended from Noah, these laws would be binding for and expected of all human beings, not just the Jews. What we would call the Jewish law today was given by Moses specifically to the Jews, not to the other nations of the world.

The seven Noahide Laws were these (there is slight variation in order and sometimes in wording in the Talmud, the Jewish commentaries where these rules are most discussed):

1. No idols.
2. No murder.
3. No robbery.

4. No sexual immorality.

5. Don't eat an animal with its lifeblood still in it.

6. No blasphemy.

7. Establish a system of justice for the people.

You may have noticed that James mentioned only three of these (with the "no idols" being modified to "do not eat food sacrificed to idols"). I suspect that is because in the Roman system, which all of the non-Jews were a part of, the other moral expectations were already in place. The Romans had a system of justice established. Murder and theft were illegal and commonly understood to be immoral. The Roman value on being an honest person (*veritas*) was strong.

Roman society's attitude toward sexual immorality, on the other hand, was one of more or less complete license to do as one pleased (especially if you were a man). Idolatry was common, and there had been questions about whether it was OK to eat food that had been dedicated to idols. Likewise, Roman attitudes toward animals were less restrictive than those of Jews (many Jewish commentators read the Noahide prohibition against eating animals with the lifeblood still in them—i.e., still alive—as indicative of a wider expectation from God that we not be cruel to animals).

Basically, James was saying, "Let's make sure the non-Jews know what is expected of them, especially in those areas that might be unclear." Now, you might be asking, "Why didn't they just say to follow the Ten Commandments?" The simple answer is that the Ten Commandments were given to the Jewish people. James, Paul, Peter, and others saw no need to expect non-Jews to obey the Ten Commandments.

I know that's probably shocking and possibly upsetting. Yes, I realize Jesus taught on the Ten Commandments, but again, he was teaching Jewish people. At the same time, I don't believe the Twelve were saying, "Oh, I don't suppose the Gentiles need to honor their parents, and it's probably OK for them to covet." Many of these things were already expected in the wider culture. The simple fact is that James and the Twelve read the Scriptures like Jewish people. They saw the law of Moses as something for the people of Israel, and they saw the new, non-Jewish believers as devout, God-loving non-Jews.

The baffling part of the whole situation was that God appeared to accept the non-Jews without reserve, gifting them with the same Holy Spirit the Jews had received. James and the leadership were not saying, "Christians don't need to follow the law because we have entered an age of grace" but rather, "Non-Jewish Christians don't need to follow the law of Moses." It's not for them; it's for the Jews. James and his leaders had every intention of continuing to follow the law and to teach their children to do so because they were Jews.

"Follow Me" versus "Follow These"

What lessons can we learn from this?

For most of us, there's a constant battle to balance following Jesus with following the rules. What we want, and what we should want for those whom we teach, is to create pure Jesus followers—people who come close to Jesus and become more like him. As we become more like Jesus, we behave more like him, thus naturally stopping sinful behavior and embracing pure, beautiful, godly behavior.

The trick, of course, is that it's nearly impossible to tell the difference between a legalist and a Jesus follower—at least from the outside. Someone following the rules may behave similarly to someone following Jesus and vice versa. But Jesus followers are disciples, learners, students. Rule followers are legalists.

For instance, someone following Jesus may choose not to lie because Jesus is the Truth. Their proximity to him, their Christlikeness, teaches them not to lie. On the other hand, someone following the rules will work hard to be honest because "lying is wrong." They're following a moral code, not following Jesus. It's a thin line, and it may be difficult, even painful, to discern which is which.

I might as well put it all out on the table. Most of us are a mix of legalist and Jesus follower. We all have places in our lives where we are following Jesus and places where we are following rules. Not that legalism is all bad. It has a valuable, useful role in our lives.

For instance, we teach our children how to be safe using legalism. Don't touch the hot stove. Don't cross the street without a parent. Don't put a fork in an electrical socket. We tell them a series of rules but don't always explain the reasoning behind them.

It's easy to teach people to follow rules. It's faster too. And it's safer. It's tempting to build our lives around rules so there aren't any questions, there's never uncertainty, and we have a measuring stick (a "ruler," so to speak) for those around us.

Let's explore how legalism works. My friend Gerry uses the metaphor of a cliff and a series of fences. "Falling into sin" is the cliff. So let's pick a sin. How about lying? Lying is a cliff. Because the cliff is dangerous, we build a little fence at the edge to keep us away from lying. Maybe our first fence is "lying is wrong," so I won't use exaggeration when telling funny stories. It's not lying, but it's pretty close.

Then we start to think, *Wow. That fence is awfully close to the cliff. I should put up another fence around the first fence.* Then another fence around that one. Then another. Depending on how far and how fast we build the fences, we can get into strange territories without noticing it.

Fence #25: I won't watch movies that aren't true.

Fence #32: I'll only read bedtime stories to children if they are true. The only book I know for sure to be true is the Bible, so that's the only book allowed at bedtime.

Fence #107: The best way to avoid lying would be to never speak aloud again.

Lying is a sin. The cliff is a legitimate risk. It's OK to be wary of it. Is it a sin to cross the fences that protect us from that sin, though? No. It's not wise, maybe, but it's not a sin. Is it OK to watch movies that aren't true? Sure. It's not a sin, at least not in and of itself.

Legalism redefines what is sin and what is not. Legalism doesn't say falling off the cliff is a sin; it calls crossing any fence a sin.

The Jews, by the way, were no strangers to this concept. Take the commandment "Do not take the name of the LORD your God in vain." Basically, this means not to use his name needlessly. For instance, don't hammer your finger and then shout God's name.

The Jews, however, began to build fences around this until they stopped saying his name (Yahweh) ever. They would write it down, but when they read it aloud, they would pronounce the word *Yahweh* (which is God's proper name) as "Adonai." God asked them not to use his name needlessly, and they never said his name again. Is it a sin to say God's name? No. Is it a sin to say his name frivolously? Yes.

Let's do one more example, and then we'll talk about how to identify legalism in our own lives.

Cliff: Sexual immorality. It's a sin to have sex outside of marriage.

OK, great! That's a cliff we should try to avoid. Let's build some fences.

Fence #1: When you're alone in a room with someone of the opposite sex, keep the door open so you know people can see inside. (A note to my daughters: this particular fence might be dictated to you by your parents!)

Fence #17: No bikinis.

Fence #30: A married man should never drive in a car alone with a single woman.

Fence #47: We need to have "guys time" and "girls time" at the camp swimming pool to make sure they don't see each other in their swimsuits.

Fence #53: You know what, maybe we should have separate sidewalks for men and women.

Is it a sin to wear a bikini? It is not. The Bible never mentions it. Those who call it immodest are making a cultural declaration, nothing more. A bikini is not inherently more or less modest than a one-piece, or a pair of tight jeans, or a nice floral dress.

Is it a sin for a married man to drive somewhere in a car with a single woman?[1] No.

Are those things wise? Maybe or maybe not. But when we call them sin, that's legalism. When we use them as litmus tests to tell whether other people are following Jesus, that's legalism. We are following rules rather than following Jesus. I'm not suggesting we go dancing along the edge of the cliff, merely that we should keep a clear idea in our mind what is actually sin and what is not. Following Jesus is about receiving a transformed heart, not about rigorous rule following and enforcing those rules on others. Legalism and transformation can both keep us away from the cliff edge, but Jesus speaks consistently of the transformed heart's superiority over the protections of legalistic moralism.

Warning: Fences Ahead

We are blind to our own legalisms. No one wants to be a legalist, so if we could see it ourselves, we'd fix it. However, with some careful observation, we can identify the places we slip into legalism.

Here are five questions I use to discover my own legalisms:

1. Do I find myself offended often in a certain area, especially when I go somewhere new (another culture, another church, another ministry)?
2. Do I have a list of "sins" that aren't in Scripture? (You're going to be tempted to say "no" without thinking. If that happens, try this question: "Which of my list of 'sins' are not specifically spelled out in Scripture?")
3. Do I catch myself thinking how much better I am than others who don't follow the same rules I do?
4. Do I find myself doing the right thing out of obligation rather than because it's something I desire?
5. Do I find that my rules are more important than being loving toward God or other people?

That fifth one is probably the most important question. Remember, when Jesus was asked for the most important commandment, he said, "Love God" and second, "Love your neighbor as yourself."

In my last book, *The First Time We Saw Him*, I told the story of an unbelieving friend of mine who went to church with me. She had piercings and dyed hair, and we were asked to leave the church because she was dressed inappropriately. I'm certain the man who asked us to leave thought he was teaching us a valuable lesson about respecting God. We had accidentally trampled one of his fences.

I do believe God desires us to approach him with respect. I don't think wearing a short skirt and having purple hair is automatically disrespectful, especially for a nonbeliever. She was curious about God and wanted to go to church, but this gentleman had a rule. If you approach God, you ought to look like someone should at church—you know, floral dress, brushed hair, light makeup, conservative shoes. She violated his rules, so she couldn't remain. The man who asked us to leave is precisely the sort of man who would have turned away the eunuch for not being masculine enough.

What do you think would have happened if he had seen my friend and made a decision based on love rather than on legalism? He would have known she was an outsider (by the fact that she didn't fit in); he would have realized she had some spiritual interest (by the fact that she had shown up at all); and instead of kicking us out, he would have engaged with us in a spiritual conversation. He would have said something as simple as, "What's your name? Why did you come to church today?"

Jesus took people to task for the same thing in his day. He mentioned legalists who used the law to their advantage to get around taking care of their parents. They followed the rules and failed to love.

Those who follow the rules instead of following Jesus wander away from the faith eventually. Some of them figure out that the rules they've been taught aren't sins in and of themselves, then they get disillusioned and wonder what else isn't true. Others keep coming to church, looking perfect, but they're hollow and empty inside. Like a beautifully ornate lawn covering graves. Like whitewashed tombs.

Those who follow Jesus, those who fall in love with him, will continue to follow even when they go through hard times, even when he asks for difficult things. Following rules does not always lead to following Jesus. On the other hand, following Jesus does lead to less sin in our lives.

The early leaders in the church thought it best to define the cliffs, put out a few signposts, and trust that the grace of the Holy Spirit would do the rest.

12

Stealing Zeus

The idols in this place. Every hallway crammed with them. Many-armed goddesses with skulls for belts. Fierce, dragon-faced warriors, and creatures with human bodies but animal heads, or the other way around. Gods from around the world, thrown together in a massive jumble of religions, like some sort of getting-to-know-you neighborhood mixer for the gods. Paul can't stand it. He paces among them, stopping to stare at them. He starts to say something, to rage about it, then catches himself and falls silent. That passion, the same passion that drove him to chase the followers of Jesus across city lines, down highways, and into obscure neighborhoods weighs on him now. "This is what they think," he says, jabbing a finger at a painting of a sharp-toothed god who is tearing human bodies in half with his mouth. "This is who they think God is."

The misunderstandings drive him crazy. Worse, he sees people in the religious community—people of his religion—buying into them. He can't keep his feelings to himself. He tears into them, publicly humiliating them. Others hear him. The city is full of pantheists. I stand beside a few of them and eavesdrop on their conversation.

"What is he going on about?" one of them asks. "The foreigner over there."

"Something about his foreign gods," says another, shrugging as if to say, "Who needs more of those?"

"I don't know," says the first. "He seems interesting. He's saying something different at least. Let's invite him to the Philosophical Society tonight."

So they do. They approach him and say several complimentary things, which Paul seems to accept, although his face twitches at a few of their words. They like that he says something new but don't seem interested in the actual message. Paul doesn't care for that. But he is never one to turn down a chance to speak, and that night he shows up at the Philosophical Society.

When it is his turn to take the stage, he takes the microphone out of its stand and walks to the very edge of the platform. He looks into the audience and says, "I've walked among the idols in this town, and I know that you're religious. In fact, I've been reading some of the Hindu Vedas, and while reading through those ancient hymns, I found something interesting. I found a hymn written to a god whose name you cannot remember. This is a line from it: 'He who by his might looked out over the waters which held power and generated light, he who alone is God above all gods: Who is this God to whom we shall offer our sacrifice?'"

Paul pauses, looking at the audience again. They don't respond, don't shout questions or interact with him, not yet. He says, "This God, the one who made light and hovered over the water, the God who is above all gods, you don't know him, but I will introduce you."

"Go on then!" a woman shouts from the crowd.

A man sitting beside me sloshes his beer and shouts, "Make the introductions!"

Paul smiles at them. I have seen this smile before. When Paul knows an audience is where he wants them, when he knows his words will drive them in the direction he wants, he gets this small, fierce smile. He looks like a dangerous animal. A jolt of electricity runs through the crowd.

"The God you don't know but have worshiped by accident doesn't live in a temple or a church."

"Not even yours?"

"I'll say it again. He doesn't live in a place made by human beings. He doesn't need anything from people. Not idols or sacrifices or even praise. He is the giver of life and breath. He started with one human being and made every nation on earth and decided where they would live and when for one reason: that each of us would try to find him. That we might grope around searching for him and perhaps come across him. It's not that he's far from any of us. As it says in the Bhagavad Gita, "All beings are in me." We move and live and do what we do and exist because we are in him. Again, your own poets say that we are all God's children."

He pauses and raises his eyebrows. No word from the crowd. He continues, "If God is our parent, then he must not be made of stone. Not even gold or silver. If he is our parent, then we can't create him, can we? We can't shape an image using our skill and imagination and say that this idol, this art, this image is God. Can we?"

There is some pushback now. People have begun to stand. A few shout questions. Not all think God is in the idols or is an idol, and they begin to shout things to him as well.

Paul doesn't pause at this moment. Instead, he raises his voice and shouts, "In the past, God overlooked our ignorance. He forgave our lack of knowledge. Now he tells all of us to turn back from our evil ways because he has circled a day on his calendar and written 'Judgment Day.' He's chosen the one who will judge us, and he's proven it by bringing that man to life after we killed him."

163

Now there is a real uproar. People are throwing snacks and cups half filled with beer along with their taunts. Saying that a man rose from the dead just took the talk from philosophical into the realm of the ridiculous. Paul tries to speak over them, but even with the microphone, they can't hear him. He raises his hands, sets the microphone down, and walks off the stage.

He pushes out of the Society doors and onto the street. A small knot of people follow. One of them, a woman named Damaris, says, "We'd like to talk with you some more."

Paul pushes his hand through his curly hair, shaking. When he speaks, the adrenaline courses through him. It will take some time for him to calm down. "Sure," he says. He blinks, as if he isn't seeing clearly. He rubs his eyes. "Of course. Get your friends, and we'll find a place. I saw a café on the way here, just down this street."

They know the place, and a small crowd meets Paul there. They talk far into the night over half-cooled cups of coffee and plates of half-eaten pie. Before the night is through, a few of them believe the story. Damaris is one of them, and a member of the Philosophical Society, and a few others. Paul returns to his hotel, throws himself on the bed without taking off his clothes, and sleeps late into the morning.

Star Wars, New Age, and the Church

When I was a kid, I fell in love with this amazing movie. It was about this guy who runs away from home and gets a laser sword and falls in love with a princess and makes friends with a smuggler and a hairball and some robots and then learns some stuff from a wizard and then fights a guy in black armor who is also a wizard and has a laser sword and in the end blows up the enemy base and gets a medal. It was amazing, and it's fair to say that over the next several years, I reoriented large parts of my grade-school life to obsessively collecting toys, books, comics, and even an alarm clock that woke me up to the sweet sound of robots telling me, "Wake up, little rebel, or you're going to be late!"

So I was deeply concerned when one day after church my parents told me that *Star Wars* had come up during the sermon that day. I was in fifth grade by now. There had been three movies, and my room was a shrine to the series. I knew that church was the place where fun things were taken away from you, so I was immediately on guard when Mom said, "The guest speaker today said some interesting things about *Star Wars*."

I looked at her out of the corner of my eye. "What kind of interesting things?"

"He said it had underpinnings of New Age philosophy."

"No it doesn't!" I shouted and burst into tears.

My parents, understandably confused, had to wait for me to stop sobbing "Don't take away my *Star Wars* toys!" before they figured it out.

"We're not taking away your toys," my mom said. "I just said it was *interesting*."

The speaker that day wasn't wrong. Well, not exactly. He was seeing Lucas's attempt to create an underlying "universal" religion for his movie universe that had aspects of Christianity and Buddhism and a few other things thrown into the stew. In fact, Lucas has described himself in the past as a "Buddhist Methodist."[1] Clearly, the "force that connects all life" and the desire to achieve a sort of serenity through the removal of desires are representative of a Buddhist mind-set. At the same time, I remember that we had this book at my house about how the gospel was revealed in *Star Wars*. It talked about various pieces of the *Star Wars* story that could be seen as reflections of the story of Jesus, including the brave sacrifice and sort-of resurrection of a character called Obi-Wan Kenobi.

This situation got me thinking about the potential differences in the responses of Jesus followers to pagan religions. Some want to sound the warning horn, shouting, "Behold! An evil religion! Protect the children!" Others, like my wonderful parents, might say, "Hmm. That's interesting. I'll keep an eye on that." Still others look at them and say, "There is some truth in them, truth that might help me explain more about Jesus."

In Acts 17, it seems that Paul might have gone through all three of these responses at some point. It began for Paul when he arrived in the city of Athens, the heart of Hellenistic culture in the world at this time. I love the description of this moment in Clinton E. Arnold's commentary on Acts. He describes Paul getting off the boat at the harbor of Piraeus and entering through the city gates. He walks in past enormous marble temples, he sees towers made of marble, he passes architecture unlike anything he has seen in his life. But he's also deeply troubled by the idols he sees on every corner, in the artwork on the buildings, crowded into the little shops along the street. Whether he's angry or full of sorrow is hard to decide, but it's clear that he has little patience for this evil.

At the same time, it's clear that Paul had some interest in the theology and philosophy of the place, as we'll see in a moment. He spent a significant amount of time studying the idols, reading the theology, watching plays, and reading poetry of the Greeks. He also saw a chance to steal all of the wonderful things in this city and use them to lead people to Christ. I mean that in a very real sense. He saw the theology of the Greeks and thought that he could crawl inside of it and take it over. He could use their religion, their belief structure, to reveal Christ to the people of Athens. He took it from them and gave them something different in return.

The Greeks were multicultural in the broadest sense of the word. They were glad to adopt new gods into their pantheon, though most people had a favorite here or there. Paul's preaching about his Eastern "gods" piqued their interest, and they invited him to speak at the Aeropagus, which when translated means "the Hill of Ares." Ares was the Greek god of war. The Romans, who ruled the world at this time, called their god of war Mars, so you'll sometimes see this translated as "Mars Hill."

At the Hill of Ares, philosophers gathered to talk and debate and share new ideas with one another. Paul was invited in as a curiosity. People were interested in what he might have to say. There were two major philosophical and religious camps at the Hill of Ares that day, the Epicureans and the Stoics (Acts 17:18). There would have been others there as well, including those who worshiped Zeus or Artemis or any number of other gods and who had a sincere belief that these were real gods, not mythological constructs or philosophical stand-ins.

Here's a brief, incredibly simplistic explanation of what the Stoics and Epicureans believed. The Stoics were pantheists, meaning that they believed God was in everything, that the universe and God were essentially identical. God permeated the universe. They might have referred to God as Zeus, but they thought most representations of the gods were but shadows reflecting the real thing: the universe itself and all the material making up that universe.

The Epicureans believed that the gods existed but were superior to humanity and therefore didn't ever really interact with human beings. There was no need to worship them or attempt to curry their favor because they would never step in to do anything. Religious reverence and ritual in general were shunned by the Epicureans.

Neither philosophy believed in any judgment after death or really in much of an afterlife. People died and returned to the elements they were made from. Interestingly, both philosophies were referred to as a form of atheism at some point during their existence—the Epicureans because their belief in a distant set of gods who never interacted with humanity created a religious framework that required no acknowledgment of a god, and the Stoics because saying that "God is everything in the universe" was essentially the same as saying that "there is no god, only the universe." It's a confusion of terms. The Stoics and the Epicureans liked to duke it out with each other, and no doubt they liked the idea that Paul might inject something new into the conversation.

Stealing Zeus

Paul started the conversation by doing something fascinating. He co-opted the religious practices and theological writings of their own theologians. It might have made you a little uncomfortable to hear Paul, in the beginning of this chapter, quoting from the Bhagavad Gita. In the Bhagavad Gita, chapter 9, text 4, Krishna says, "By me, in my unmanifested form, this entire universe is pervaded. All beings are in me, but I am not in them." I also had Paul quote from an ancient Hindu praise song called a Veda. It's from the Mandala, Veda number 121. It's a fascinating song written for "an unknown god." Throughout the song, the singer describes this god, who made the seas and created light and designed the skies, and then asks what his name is so they can address him when they make their sacrifices.

Would we quote from the Bhagavad Gita in our churches? Would we equate the Lord Jesus with Krishna? Should we be singing Hindu praise songs in the Christian church?

I doubt Paul would sign off on that. Nevertheless, in Acts 17, he did something interesting. He started by mentioning the altar to an unknown god. He used this as a way to start the conversation. He told them that he could inform them about the unknown god. Then he quoted some Stoic philosophers.

There are two quotations here that Paul used to illuminate the one true God. You've heard them many times, I'm sure. "In him we live and move and have our being" and "We are all God's offspring."

The first quotation comes from Epimenides's poem *Cretica*. In this poem, a character named Minos has written a sort of eulogy for Zeus, who some are saying is dead. But Minos says:

> They fashioned a tomb for you, holy and high one,
> Cretans, always liars, evil beasts, slow bellies.
> But you are not dead. You live and abide forever,
> For in you we live and move and have our being.

That's right. In Paul's speech, he referred to how we live, move, and have our being in God. But the god of the poem was *Zeus*.

Likewise, the quotation saying "We are all God's offspring" comes from a poem called *Phaenomena* by Aratus.

> Let us begin with Zeus, whom we mortals never leave unspoken.
> For every street, every market-place is full of Zeus.
> Even the sea and the harbor are full of this deity.
> Everyone everywhere is indebted to Zeus.
> For we are his offspring.[2]

Zeus! Paul was talking about Zeus? He was there to tell the Greeks about his unique philosophy, his strange foreign God, and what did he do? He began by equating the one true God with the head of the Greek pantheon (or, for the Stoics, with the god who is everything). There's no way around it. Paul was quoting from pagan poetry and philosophy, which means he had not only read it but also memorized it. He had looked into it pretty extensively. He was connecting the true God to the current pagan beliefs of his listeners.

What does this mean for us?

First of all, it means that we should not be afraid to study other religions. There can be a fear that those religions will contaminate or destroy Christian belief. But if you're ministering to Hindus, doesn't it show respect to them and their beliefs if you know about Hinduism? Doesn't it show you are equals if you learn about their religion as you teach them about yours?

Paul learned about Greek religion, and it appears that he studied it, looking for theological common ground. He wanted to find places where the Greek religion had true insights into theological things. Then he held up those places and said, "Aha! So we agree on this. That's a great theological insight. I agree with that one!"

So with a Hindu, we can talk about the unknown god who created light while hovering over the water. With a Muslim, we can discuss the Qur'an, which says that the "holy" Jesus was born to his mother, Mary, who was a virgin.[3] With a Wiccan, we can agree that nature is something beautiful and revelatory. Even with an atheist, we can discuss theological insights where we agree: the importance of humanity, maybe, or that the universe as we know it started with light exploding into darkness.

It's not that the conversation ends there or that we're allowing other religions to dictate our own. It's that we're sorting through two belief systems and finding the places they overlap and starting the conversation there.

Now, Paul didn't stop with comparing similarities. As his speech progressed, he brought up things that the Greek philosophers found ridiculous: the resurrection and Jesus as God. The point is not merely to say "Oh, we agree with one another," but to move on from that to "Here are some things about God on which we disagree." There will be some who mock from the audience and others who say, "I want to hear more about that."

The major point is this: Paul was not afraid to know his audience's religion and philosophy well so that he could use their own terminology, insights, and beliefs to move them closer to the one true God. We can do the same, whether it's religion or pop culture or a certain type of music or a movie that young people are obsessing over.

I used to be the kind of guy who went into bookstores and tried to hide certain books I found dangerous or misleading. Now I realize that God is stronger than those things and that he can be found even on dangerous pathways. If someone is drawn to the dark, I don't need to block access to dark and dangerous places. I need to follow after them and bring them the light.

I'm glad to say my parents didn't take away my *Star Wars* toys. That may have been a wise solution for some kids, but it wasn't for me. We had an illuminating discussion about life, religion, and how to follow Jesus and be in the world but not of the world. Then the *Star Wars* prequels came along, and I just naturally grew out of it.

Those places where truth appears in a false religion, in pop culture, in politics, or in literature are places where Christ reveals himself to all who come. Christ reveals himself there because he is the truth, and all truth leads inexorably toward him.

One More Reminder

One last thought. Sometimes I find myself crippled with fear or uncertainty about telling people about Jesus. Sometimes I talk myself out of it, hiding behind a lot of theological and practical smoke screens. Sometimes I say that it wouldn't be "culturally relevant" in that moment to talk to someone.

What have I forgotten in those moments?

I've forgotten that this book is not "The Acts of the Apostles." It's the story of the Holy Spirit proclaiming the good news to humanity. He's at work in situations I have never imagined (like the young Buddhist man in chapter 8). I love when Paul says:

> From one man he made all the nations, that they should inhabit the whole earth; and he marked out their appointed times in history and the boundaries of their lands. God did this so that they would seek him and perhaps reach out for him and find him, though he is not far from any one of us. (Acts 17:26–27)

Paul tells us that God has chosen the times and places when and where all the people of the world live. Why? To give them the best possible chance to look for him, to try to find him, to stumble through the dark looking for his light. I don't need to worry when I talk to someone that "maybe they don't want to hear." Instead, I should wonder if perhaps they are intersecting with my life because maybe, just maybe, I have been blessed with the opportunity to help them seek and find God.

This concept came powerfully to life for me once when I took a trip to Costa Rica. While there, my friend Adena and I went out on the campus of Universidad de Costa Rica to talk with some students about Jesus. I speak only "restaurant Spanish," which means I can say things like, "Mas burritos por favor." Adena's Spanish at that time was limited as well.

We randomly chose a group of studying students and asked them if they wanted to talk about spiritual things. They said yes. We used a gospel tract to share some spiritual truths with them. I know, I know, I've heard that they don't work and that they do more harm than good too. But that wasn't my experience. The tract was in Spanish and had a variety of simple sentences coupled with Bible verses. Basically, it taught things like God loves you; people are sinful, and that sin separates them from God; Jesus is the only way to overcome sin and be connected to God.

After the students had finished reading the booklet, we asked each of them what they thought of the content. One said it was nothing new; she had heard it all before. Another said she didn't believe it but thought it was interesting. The third said, "Every night I lie in bed and I pray. I say, 'God, if you are real, please show yourself to me.' Every night I pray this, but he doesn't answer."

We asked what she thought of the little book. She said, "I believe you talking to me today is the answer to my prayers."

God has chosen the exact time and place when and where everyone lives so that they might, maybe, perhaps, reach out for him and find him. Your neighbors. Your roommates. Your co-workers. Your family. Strangers walking by on a crowded street.

And we, God's spokespeople, just like Paul, have an opportunity to be an answer to their prayers.

13

Upside Down

When Governor Agrippa arrives, it's with a great deal of ceremony. Red carpets. Spotlights. Limousines. His sister, Bernice, is with him, wearing an evening gown. Many of the most important businesspeople in the city have shown up as well, and the state CFO, Mr. Festus, has put together a party designed to impress at his own mansion. The governor and his retinue have a table set up on a small stage facing the floor where presentations will be made. The governor's sister sits on one side of him, Mr. Festus on the other.

I'm invited to the party. Because I'm a doctor and a traveler, Mr. Festus thinks I'll bring some interesting flavor to the conversations in the room. I'm seated on the floor near where Paul will speak. This isn't just a party; Festus wants to do a little business as well.

Governor Agrippa is an influential, important man. He was more than a governor not long ago but was ousted, then given his post as governor. He's thankful for that, at least. He's rich. Well connected. He has a light curl to his hair, which perches just on the crown of his head. He has a weak chin, which makes the rest of his face look as if it juts forward, as if he's leaning in. He looks perpetually fascinated by the world in front of him.

Before bringing Paul out, Mr. Festus gives a small refresher on his case. How a crowd was beating him to death upon the stairs of the church, and how the National Guard had rolled out from their bunker to break things up. How Paul had convinced the military to let him speak to the crowd, which had sent them into a violent frenzy. How he had been arrested, his face swollen and bleeding, and kept in a series of cells, while the mob howled and raged outside.

When it was finally decided to move Paul, a group of men plotted to kill him, and the soldiers had moved him in the middle of the night, complete with armored personnel carriers and armed guards. No one knew what to do with him, and in the middle of a particularly intense legal battle, Paul had demanded that his case be remanded to the Supreme Court.

Mr. Festus had agreed to send him along, the only problem being that he was uncertain what legal grounds there were even to hold him. As far as he could tell, there was no reason he should have been arrested and certainly no reason for him to face the death penalty, which is what Paul's enemies demand.

Mr. Festus asks those present to consider Paul's case carefully and to help him decide what to communicate to his superiors when he kicks Paul up the chain. Then he brings the prisoner out.

It has been two years since Paul was arrested, but when he makes his defense (again), it's as if he's doing it for the first time. He's a natural orator, and when he stands to speak, he stands straight, he stands tall. His orange jumpsuit is no distraction. The handcuffs on his hands make his motions less natural, perhaps, than would be normal for him, but the passion in his voice and the sincere look in his eye more than make up for it.

He begins by complimenting the authorities gathered to hear from him. He tells them about his childhood, about how he was reared to be a Bible-believing, devout, passionate scholar of God. He pauses briefly to expound on the wondrous God he serves and to compliment those who also serve him well. "If we believe in a God such as this," he says, "why should it seem incredible that such a God could bring the dead back to life?"

I can see Mr. Festus crinkle his nose at that. He believes that when death comes, all is done. The thought of a life after life rankles him.

Paul continues. "I saw it as my solemn duty to oppose the name of this upstart cult leader, Jesus from Nazareth. I arrested his followers. I worked hard to get them to deny him, to admit publicly that he was not God—as I would say now, to blaspheme by denying his divinity." He lifts his hands, the cuffs clinking against his wrists. "When they went on trial, I hoped for their deaths."

Governor Agrippa leans over and says something to Mr. Festus.

"I was on the road," he says. "A new town loomed on the horizon full of these Jesus followers. The authority to arrest and remove them resided in my breast pocket in the form of orders from our religious leaders. I, and those with me, drove with righteous confidence."

Governor Agrippa shifts in his seat. He looks at Bernice and then squeezes her hand lightly before returning it to the arm of his chair. I wonder if his attention is wandering. Paul must wonder also, because he uses the man's name in his next sentence.

"Around noon, Governor Agrippa, while still on the road, a bright light came from heaven. I put down the sun visor, but the light only increased. My sunglasses did nothing. The vast white burning grew so intense that I stopped the car. I couldn't see anything. I threw open the car door and stumbled into the road, holding my hand above my eyes, trying to shield myself somehow from the glare. It was as if the light had weight. I couldn't stand in its presence, and I found myself falling to my knees."

Paul pauses here, as if searching for words, though I have heard him tell this story many times. At last, he gestures to a guitar on the side of the stage. "Imagine the whole world as a guitar string," he says. "It's as if some great hand came down and strummed the string of the universe. The vibrations from that unseen hand echoed out into the world. I stood at the center of it, and I had a singular experience. Those beside me, just outside the epicenter of the event, heard the sounds and saw the light, but they did not hear what I heard. And what was it that I heard?"

He clears his throat. "A voice. An ordinary, human voice that spoke in the language of my home country. A voice that could have been the voice of my neighbor as a child, and he used the name my mother had given me, which she called me my entire boyhood. 'Saul,' he said. 'Saul. Why do you harass me? Why are you mistreating me? You are harming yourself, like a man who grips the blade of a sharp knife in his fist. Why would you do that?'"

Everyone is listening now. The governor has definitely leaned forward in his seat, and his eyes are unquestionably fastened on Paul's. He steeples his fingers and places them on his lips. Paul holds his arm up, as if warding off that burning light, and says, his voice trembling, "I asked him, 'Who are you, sir?' The voice replied, as if I should have known, 'I am Y'shua. The one you are mistreating. Now stand up.'

"I stood. The voice said, 'I have come to you today because from now on you will do as I say. You work for me now. You will tell others what you have seen here and what I will show you in the future. I will rescue you from your own people and from foreigners. I'm sending you to them to turn them from the darkness and toward the light, to release them from Satan's influence and move them toward God so that they can be forgiven of the terrible things they have done and find a home among my people, those who have been washed clean by believing in me.'

"I have not been disobedient to that vision from heaven," Paul says. Then he shares what he has seen at home and abroad. He preached in the churches and in the streets. What did he preach? That people should turn toward God and prove it by their actions. This is why religious leaders hate him. This is why people tried to kill him. "But God has helped me," Paul says, "and continues to do so today. I am not saying anything that doesn't already appear in the Bible: our Savior was destined to suffer, and, as the first one to die and come back to life, he would publicly make the way of light known to all of humanity."

Mr. Festus, finally, can take it no longer and half shouts, "You're mad. Clearly you've studied hard and gotten your doctorate, but somewhere in those stacks of dusty books you lost the plot. You're insane."

Paul pauses as if in midthought. "My dear Mr. Festus," he says. "On the contrary, I'm a sane and logical man, and what I am saying is both true and reasonable." He lowers his arms and bows his head slightly toward Agrippa. "The governor knows about these things, and I can speak my mind without self-editing. He's noticed these things already; this isn't anything new to him. It wasn't done behind closed doors."

There is silence in the room. No one stirs; no one speaks. There is not so much as a rustle of cloth. Paul takes two steps forward. "Governor Agrippa, do you believe the words of God's prophets?" Agrippa does not speak. "I know that you do."

Agrippa stares at him, as if in a trance, and then shakes his head, his eyes blinking. He cuts the conversation short with a simple chop of his flattened hand. "Do you think that in one ten-minute speech you will convince me to follow your Jesus?"

Paul nods as if conceding a point. "Ten minutes or ten years. I pray to God that you and everyone in this room will become like me." He holds up his hands. "Except for these cuffs."

At that, Governor Agrippa stands, along with Bernice and Mr. Festus and the entire company. Without another word, they take their leave, and I follow quickly behind, turning only to see the prison guards take hold of Paul's elbows to lead him back to his cell. After they leave the main ballroom, the governor drifts back and takes Mr. Festus by the elbow. "This man shouldn't even be in jail," he says.

"Certainly not," Mr. Festus says. "In a society like ours, there is freedom to be a little crazy. His religious beliefs are not enough to make him a threat to the government. I'd like to release him."

"You can't," Agrippa says. "He's already entered himself into the legal system. To cut him loose now is impossible. You have to send him along to the Supreme Court. He'll have to remain imprisoned for now. Send him on to the capital."

A Sermon in Chains

Paul's story, more than anyone else's, shows how the early followers of Jesus turned the world upside down. Everywhere he went, life-changing chaos ensued, starting with himself on the road to Damascus. The light blinded him, and when he opened his eyes again, he saw a new world, with Christ as his master instead of as the object of his hate.

He entered new towns, and some came to follow the way of Jesus, but others tried to murder him. People fought him, afraid they'd lose their livelihood, their way of life, their positions, their power, their gods, their influence, and it happened in nearly every city Paul visited. Sometimes it happened on his first day in town, sometimes after he'd been visiting for a while. As the world got more and more stirred up, Paul was praying peacefully in the temple, bothering no one, not even preaching, when a bloodthirsty mob formed at the suggestion that he was in town.

After being beaten half to death and rescued by the Roman soldiers, Paul asked to speak to the crowd and got them riled up so badly that a group of men took a vow not to eat or drink until they managed to murder him. I suppose they died thirsty, because Paul's nephew heard about the plan and warned the soldiers, who rallied the guard in the middle of the night and whisked Paul away.

In the rest of this chapter, we'll look at three observations about the core of the early Christian's world-spinning theology, each taken from Paul's speech before King Agrippa, Bernice, and Proconsul Festus in Acts 26. These were, incidentally, the most influential people Paul preached to in the book of Acts. It's interesting to note that, unlike most of the times Paul shared the good news, no one in his audience appeared to respond to the message. I do like the moment when Paul said, "Do you believe in the prophets? I know that you do." Obviously, if Agrippa agreed that he believed in the prophets, Paul had the upper hand. He knew the prophets well and could convincingly show how their prophecies led to Jesus. But Agrippa declined to continue the conversation.

A Simple Message with Complicated Results

The first observation is this: Paul shared the message that had been given to him, not what had been entrusted to other people.

As I wrote this book, one thing that troubled me about Paul was the lack of references he made to the teachings of Jesus. Though he often taught about the crucifixion and resurrection, he rarely directly spoke about Jesus's teachings in his earthly ministry. One clear place he talks about Jesus's earthly teaching is 1 Corinthians 11:23–26, when referencing the Lord's Supper. Compelling cases can be made that other comments of Paul came from an awareness of the teachings of Jesus,[1] but regardless, I found myself troubled that he never, for instance, quoted from the Sermon on the Mount.

Why didn't he ever bring up the Lord's Prayer? Why doesn't he mention Jesus being tempted in the wilderness, or the transfiguration?

You could say he didn't have a lot of access to those materials, but that seems unlikely since he palled around with Luke, the author of the Gospel of Luke. He never mentioned Peter walking on water, or the feeding of the five thousand, or the resurrection of Lazarus.

There are a lot of theories about why this might be, and most of them reveal more about the theorist than they do about Paul, because the fact is we simply aren't sure. It's possible that he often quoted Jesus in person but not in letters. Or that he thought it confused things for him to tell the stories that the Twelve could share as eyewitnesses. Or maybe Paul didn't know all those stories or didn't think they were as important as the Old Testament prophecies, which he knew better anyway.

I think, no matter what the case may be, that Paul's decision to speak more about his experience on the Damascus road than about Peter receiving a miraculous catch of fish may well boil down to what Jesus said to Paul in his vision. In Acts 26:16, the risen Jesus said this to Paul: "I have appeared to you to appoint you as a servant and as a witness of what you have seen and will see of me."

Jesus chose Paul as a servant. In other words, to do as he was told. He also chose him to be a witness of what *he* had seen of Jesus—not what others had seen of him but what Paul had personally experienced of Jesus.

Paul was not called to be an all-knowing theologian and gatekeeper of all knowledge about Jesus. Paul was called to share what he personally had experienced of Jesus and to share the observations that Jesus gave to him. This was a powerful and freeing mission. And that's what he did: Paul shared the world-changing message of Jesus over and over through the lens of his own story. He shared the truth of Jesus by sharing how he himself became a part of the community of Jesus followers. Paul's mission was more detailed than that, of course. The point of sharing his own experience was that people would be rescued from the darkness and be able to turn from Satan toward Jesus. Why did God want them to turn to him? So that they could receive forgiveness for their sins and find a place among God's people.

I think it's significant, by the way, that no one else on the Damascus road heard God's instructions to Paul. They saw the light and heard a sound, but they didn't hear the words. Why should they? Those instructions were not for them; they were for Paul. Too often we want other people to be held accountable to the instructions God has given us as individuals.

A second observation is this: When Paul looked at why people wanted to kill him (specifically this latest time), he saw the essential infuriating message as this: "Repent and turn to God and demonstrate [your] repentance by [your] deeds" (Acts 26:20). He also said more than once that people were trying to get rid of him because he believed in the resurrection (26:6–8 being the local example).

There are plenty of places where Paul boiled down the good news to one thing or another, but it's instructive that Paul believed the part that really got everyone riled up was the idea of the resurrection of the dead and the idea that we should turn away from evil, toward God, and change our behavior.

Even in the conversation with Festus, these issues played out. Festus clearly disliked the idea of the resurrection and was driven to shout at Paul that his great learning had driven him insane (an insult I hope to personally receive someday). And it's possible that Agrippa was hesitant to hear the rest of Paul's speech because of his own sin issues (a common rumor at the time was that he and his sister were lovers).

It's amazing to think that, with the Holy Spirit's empowerment, a few simple sentences were enough to shake the foundations of the mightiest human institutions and impact historical events in a way that we're still talking about two thousand years later. "Jesus, the Savior of the world, was killed and rose from the dead. Now turn to God and show it by your actions."

The third observation is another simple one. When Festus accused Paul of being insane for believing in the resurrection, Paul didn't back down or get defensive or blush or backpedal. He simply said he was not insane and that his beliefs were "true and reasonable" (Acts 26:25).

Paul famously says in the beginning of the book of Romans that he is "not ashamed of the good news," and that's clear in this story. Also, throughout Acts, we're told that the way to share the good news is with boldness (4:29; 9:28; 14:3; 18:26; 19:8; 28:31). If I had been in Paul's place and someone with the power to release me from prison had shouted that my belief in Jesus's resurrection made me crazy, I might have been tempted to say, "Uh, hey. We all have differences of opinions. Maybe I'm right, maybe I'm wrong."

Not Paul. He pushed back and simply told Festus that he was mistaken.

It's easy in this modern world to find ourselves embarrassed by some of the core beliefs of Christianity. Virgin birth? Seems unlikely. Miracles? Umm, maybe not. People rising from the dead? Well, it hasn't happened lately.

But what did Paul say? "If there is a God as great as I believe there is, why should anyone have a problem with the idea that he occasionally brings the dead back to life? Why wouldn't he? Why couldn't he? You have an issue with the idea of the risen Jesus? I've seen him."

May God grant us the ability to speak the good news we have experienced without embarrassment, with boldness, and with simplicity.

14

The Story Tellers

Theo,

One thing that has struck me throughout this project is that we all tell our own stories best. Paul never tells the story of Peter and the miraculous catch of fish. Peter never tells the story of Paul's blinding encounter with the Risen One.

In all my interviews, as I've worked to decide which stories to include and which to throw out, I've come over and over to this question: Whose story is this?

As you know, in my first book, the hero was unquestionably the Teacher. And as I write this one, I find over and over that the hero is the Comforter, the Advocate, the Counselor who has been sent to us, the Holy Spirit.

My own story isn't worthy of inclusion among these tales. I don't want the attention of these stories to shift toward me, don't want to risk the possibility that I might find myself the center of the story somehow, when I know I am merely a bit player in the unfolding theater of God's magnificent communications to the human race.

But you know it well enough, and though I won't include it in the book to come, stories call for stories. A well-told story invites another, and hearing the wandering beauty of my brothers and sisters as they share their stories makes me want to share mine, if only for a moment.

As you know, I have studied all my life to be a doctor. From the earliest time I can remember, I have been fascinated by the way a body is put together, the things that affect it, the careful balances that create health, that cause growth, that bring long and enjoyable life.

One evening I arrived at the emergency room to see a man piled outside the door, more rags than man. I called for a gurney, and the orderlies wheeled him inside. He had been beaten badly, one eye swollen shut and purple. Three broken ribs. One leg was shattered. He smiled and thanked me as I sewed his face, and I saw he would need a dentist. He laughed when I said it, laughed and laughed and said through his swollen lips, "I thank God I still have a mouth to speak the good news about Jesus, the Savior of the world."

He was not a man for subtlety. Not in that sort of situation at least. I had worked on a thousand victims such as him, so I paid no attention to his delusional response. The human brain, when in pain, does away with social niceties and says what it pleases. I said to him, "I don't know what happened to you, friend, but I'd steer clear of those people in the future."

He spat. "I am not afraid of them." His one open eye tracked over to my face. "Good doctor," he said, "I can see that you are a man who cares deeply about healing the broken."

"That's true," I said. "The world has pain enough."

"And to be a doctor, you must care deeply about the inner workings of the world."

"Certainly," I said, pulling the suture tight and snipping it off. "Nature is a majestic and beautiful thing. It pleases me to learn more about her."

His eye flickered, struggling to stay open. "I have good news for you," he said. "Good news." His eye closed, and he slept.

I watched him, his battered face completely at peace. What could he mean? I chided myself for asking the question. The man was out of his mind, clearly.

A knife wound came at that moment, so I left him to rest. But his words haunted me throughout the night. Good news? What could it be? It bothered me more than it should have, as if an invisible finger poked me every time I managed to stop thinking about it. *Good news.*

At the end of my shift, I returned to see him sitting up in bed, in considerable pain and trying to convince a nurse that if she would bring him a crutch he would be on his way. I pulled up a stool and looked him over carefully, assuring him that he was not ready to be released.

"Dr. Lucas," he said, my first indication that he had, indeed, been fully aware earlier, "I have good news for you." Never shy about long, uninterrupted monologues, the man launched into a story of such astonishing detail I could not doubt its veracity. How he, an educated man, had seen a vision, had been blinded, had been healed, had been made aware of a God who not only loved humanity but also had come to us to prove it. A God who had plans to heal the world. "The Great Physician" he called him, and as he said those words, they entered into my heart like a knife. All of my faculties flared to life, and I turned my full attention on this man. I examined him and cross-examined him, and when that was done, I interrogated him. I did not let him rest.

He was ecstatic. He showed no signs of madness, and his story was largely self-consistent. I began to ask him question after question about this God, and then about this Jesus. Some questions he would answer in eloquent speeches, others he would dismiss with a sentence. Some questions, especially those about the earthly days of Jesus, he would answer with his eyes closed and his head back against the pillow. "You really should talk to Peter," he would say, or, "That's a good question for Mary."

That was the moment that began my journey. A life seeking a better way, a desire to be a better physician, and an encounter in the emergency room. That is how I became a follower of Jesus. And of course, dear Theo, it was you who encouraged me to go find out more for us, to gather the stories, to hear them firsthand and write them down before those first witnesses are lost to us, whether to old age or to the hands of our adversaries.

How funny it is to me that this mercurial, intelligent, infuriating man should be the one to bring me to peace with the Creator. How ironic that he has become one of my greatest friends.

This is my story. I met a broken man in an emergency room who told me there was a God who loved me and had a plan to heal the world. I knew myself that I was sick in my spirit and in need of a physician. Paul gave me a referral. Since that day, I have come to know for myself the man Jesus, the Son of God, the Holy One, who died upon a cross (as is widely known and attested to by all I have interviewed) and who stood up from his grave, showing his power over death (again, corroborated by many witnesses). He did these things so that we can know God, know repentance, and know forgiveness.

I am free, Theo!

I tell this story when I am able. I trust you will continue to tell your story as well. I pray it will be with boldness, as it should be. May the Holy Spirit teach you and speak through you.

Your great friend,
Dr. Lucas

The Story Tellers

This whole thing started fifty days after Jesus's resurrection. It started with a person and an event. The person was the Holy Spirit. The event was the people of God standing up and telling their stories, empowered by that same Spirit. The Holy Spirit made their stories understandable, and as a result, thousands of people came to God, met the Holy Spirit, interacted with Jesus, and had stories of their own.

There are times when we are tempted to tell other people's stories instead of our own. Telling stories that belong to others can be valuable. Luke did this, clearly, as he traveled the world gathering the stories of Jesus for his book and then again for his second book. He said he wanted an accurate picture. He didn't want to hear the stories secondhand. So his story was about gathering the stories of others. John sometimes shared the stories of other people. Notice how he was the only one to tell the story of Peter's restoration with Jesus after the resurrection (John 21:15–25). But even then, John was there, lingering in the background as Jesus and Peter spoke. And afterward, when Peter looked at John and asked Jesus, "What about him?" Jesus said, "What is that to you?" and told him to pay attention to his own story.

We should tell our own stories. We've noted this already in previous chapters about Paul: he almost never referenced someone else's story. He didn't mention Peter or Matthew or John or any of the Twelve, telling the stories of how they met Jesus and walked with him for three years. In his letters, Paul rarely referenced the teachings of Jesus that he would have heard from Peter and James, though he often shared the words Jesus shared with him on the road.

Maybe it's as simple as this: Paul decided to tell his own story.

Our stories matter. We all know that a witness is someone who saw something. And as John said, our story is the story of what we have seen, what we have heard, what we have looked at, and what our hands have touched.

Let's start, then, with our own story.

The people of God should be story tellers. I love the Jewish saying that God created humanity because he loves stories. What a beautiful idea. I believe everyone knows how to tell a good story. We do it naturally when we talk about events in our own lives or the day we just had. We reject poorly done or incomplete stories as irrelevant. When we say a movie is "forgettable," we often mean there was nothing worth reflecting on in the story.

I'm going to share in this next section about story structure. I'll keep it simple, so hang in there for the end when we'll see how this applies to our own everyday lives. Let's explore what it looks like to tell our own stories.

A Word about Story

I was a creative writing major in college, and we spent a lot of time sitting around talking about story: what it is, how it works, what a good story is, why there are bad stories, whether there is an objective standard sufficient to make it clear which is which. We read each other's stories, we experimented, we read great literature, we read poetry, we spun out half-true recountings of our weekends to see what caused the eyes of our classmates to light up.

When it comes to theories about what a story is, there are plenty. People have been discussing this for millennia. Aristotle spent a significant amount of time talking about this. In recent years (recent compared to Aristotle, at least), a guy named Robert McKee became all the rage in Hollywood with his book *Story*. If you've read Donald Miller's book about story, you'll see that he uses McKee's work as a springboard for his discussions about living a good story.

For simplicity's sake, I'm going to suggest that we look at the structure provided by a gentleman named Gustav Freytag. One of the things I love about Freytag is that he actually wrote compelling stories. Some story theorists are just that: people with a theory who are experiencing stories but not telling them. Freytag was a bestselling novelist, a playwright, and a critic in Germany. He was well respected by his peers, and both his novels and plays were popular among the people.

Especially in his plays, Freytag broke things down into a five-act story structure. I'm going to explain the five pieces, then we'll do an example or two, and then we'll practice with our own stories.

Act 1: the preliminary situation. Basically, this means the world we know before the story starts, things we need to be aware of, a brief introduction to characters and the situation. So, for instance, "Once upon a time there was a little girl who lived with her mother in the woods. Her name was Little Red Riding Hood." Those two sentences themselves are not much of a story. But they let us know the world of the story and the people who will be in the story.

Act 2: the initial incident. This is the event that gets the story going. It drives all the action to come. This is the moment when Little Red's mom sits her down and says, "Your grandmother is sick, and I want you to take this basket of food to her. Remember to stick to the path, and don't talk to anyone along the way." If her mother decided, for instance, to drive the food to Grandma, or to tag along with Red, or to order a pizza to be delivered to Grandma, there would be no story. The story requires Red to go alone, into the woods, headed to Grandma's house.

Act 3: crises. There are crises in a story, problems that come up for the hero. She might be defeated, or she might overcome each crisis, but regardless, there are problems she must face, one way or another. For Red, it would be things like this: a wolf tries to speak to her. Should she respond? She wasn't supposed to say anything to strangers, but he's so friendly! She decides to speak to him and instantly faces another crisis. The wolf suggests she go off the path (she's not supposed to!) and get some flowers for Grandmother. Which is a good idea. So she follows the wolf's advice and heads off the path. The wolf, delighted, gleefully runs along to grandmother's house to prepare for act 4.

Act 4: the climax. The climax is the high point of the story. It's the biggest problem the hero faces. Again, she can succeed or fail, but the problem must be faced. A story in which the hero overcomes all odds might be a comedy, and when she fails, it may be a tragedy, but either way, she must grapple with her enemy at this point of the story.

For Red, sadly, the climax is the dawning horror as she realizes that her grandmother is hairier, uglier, and more lupine than she remembered. When she suddenly realizes that her grandmother is actually the wolf in disguise, this story reaches its climax. Red can overcome her problem at this point in the story (she reaches into the food basket she brought for Grandma, pulling out the mace that her mother had wisely packed for her), or she can be overcome herself (the wolf eats her). Either way, the climax is the height of the story. Now all that remains is to wrap things up.

Act 5: the denouement. Hey, let's get a French word in here. Why not? *Denouement* is a French word that means "unraveling." This is the moment when the "knot" of the story comes undone. All loose ends are accounted for. It's also called the "falling action" as we move from the high tension of the climax into the calm of whatever happens next. Aristotle, of course, simply called this "the end."

Little Red's denouement is interesting. She has failed at every step along the way. She disobeyed her mother twice when faced with different crises and barely got out a squeak of protest when the wolf decided to eat her. Her story should probably end with, "And then the wolf dragged himself out to lay beneath a tree. He drowsed in the dappled sunlight and slowly digested his meal."

Instead, we get a surprise. A woodcutter happens along, hears the sound of the altercation at Grandma's (or hears the wolf smacking his lips; it doesn't really matter which), and arrives just in time to cut the wolf's stomach open and pull Red and Grandma out of the wolf's tummy. Hooray!

This is a special kind of story ending called the *deus ex machina*, which means "the god out of the machine." It's a term from Greek theater (translated into Latin by the Romans) where at the end of the play a god happens along and fixes everything: punishes the evildoers, rewards the just, and ties everything up in a pretty bow despite the actions of the players on the stage.

Let's look at the story structure again, this time using the story of Saul.

Act 1 (preliminary situation): Saul, a well-educated Pharisee, lives in Jerusalem.

Act 2 (initial incident): Saul watches with approval as a member of a sect is murdered because of his unwillingness to recant that Jesus is the Messiah. Pleased with the outcome, Saul decides that he will hunt down everyone from this sect and keep Judaism pure.

Act 3 (crises): Crisis 1, the Christians begin to flee Jerusalem, trying to get away from the justice Saul brings on them. They are outside his authority.

Crisis 2, Saul must convince the authorities to allow him to chase them outside the bounds of Jerusalem. (Saul triumphs over both of these crises.)

Act 4 (climax): Saul sets out for the city of Damascus, determined to continue his campaign against the Christians, when he is accosted on the road by God himself in the form of Jesus. Saul fails to overcome and is blinded and humiliated.

Act 5 (denouement): A man comes and prays for Saul, and his sight is restored. He is transformed into a Christian himself.

Bringing the Truth of the Good News into Our Stories

You'll notice that whenever Paul tells his story, it follows the basic pattern outlined above. He tells us a small bit about himself. That he is a Pharisee and a devout Jew. That he persecuted the Christians. Then he tells how Jesus met him on the road, how he was healed, and how he now works for all humanity to know Jesus. He also interprets the story for us by giving us some details about who Jesus is. He infuses his story with the good news. He doesn't just tell us the story; he tells us why the story matters.

You'll see newscasters do this. They tell us how we should feel about a story or explain its significance to us. Something like, "Politician X died today. She was raised in poverty before making her millions on the stock market. She went on to become a ferocious advocate for the poor in the United States and a senator for six years. This is a sad day for all of us." Here's what happened. Here's her story. Here's why it matters. Here's how you should feel.

How do we layer the good news into our stories? It doesn't have to be "preachy" (though it can be—preach away if that's your preference). It can be as simple as thinking through the points of the good news you're telling and making sure they are represented in some way. Let's start with these: God loves humanity. Human beings are broken and sinful. Jesus is the Messiah and came to repair humanity and bring us into God's presence.

Now, take the story of the Samaritan woman at the well in John 4. Let's review her story and then see how we can inject the good news into it.

Preliminary situation: A Samaritan woman goes out to the well to get water for her household for the day.

Initial incident: A Jewish man is resting beside the well. He shouldn't interact with a Samaritan or be alone with a woman, but he does both of those things. He asks her for a drink of water.

Crises: She begins to argue with and test him. She says that he is a Jew and she's surprised he's willing to talk to her even for a drink. He says he has water and if she knew who he was she'd want it for herself. He explains that it's living water. She says she wants to know more about that, and he tells her to get her husband and they'll all talk about it together.

Climax: The woman is not married, but she's ashamed of her current situation. She has to decide what to do about it. We know from the story that she attempts to evade the climax by not quite lying. Jesus sees through her and astonishes her by saying things about her that he should not know.

Denouement: The Jewish man claims to be the Savior of the world. She runs home to tell her family and friends.

Now, imagine the woman telling her friends the story of her experience. How would she retell it, infusing it with the good news? Maybe something like this: "I went out to the well in the heat of the day and saw a Jewish man lounging there in the sun and dust. I determined to ignore him, as they always ignore us, but he shocked me by not only paying attention to me but also speaking to me and then asking for water."

She's got her audience of fellow Samaritans hooked already. A Jew who wants to interact with us? What's going on? (This showed God's love for her. Jesus loved her enough to start the conversation.)

"I began to argue with him and pointed out that he shouldn't even be talking to me. As the conversation continued, he told me that he had water better than ours, living water. I told him I wanted some, and he said to bring my husband back and we could talk."

Probably her friends and neighbors know the story. She's been married several times and is now living with a man she's not married to. "I told him I wasn't married, and he said, 'That's very true. You've been married several times, and the man you're with now is not your husband.'" In John, it says that she said, "Come, see a man who told me everything I ever did" (4:29). (She is sinful and broken.)

"I told him I know that when the Messiah comes he'll explain everything to us. Then he said, 'I am he.'" (Jesus is the Messiah and came to bring all humanity, including Samaritans, to himself.)

Here's her story. A Jewish man interacted with her (showed he cared about her). He told her everything she had ever done (revealing that he knew her to be sinful). He told her that he was the Savior of the world (come to provide healing and to bring humanity into a relationship with God).

Sharing Our Own Story

OK, let's try it with your story. First, you need to pick which part of your story you want to tell. It doesn't have to be your conversion story (although if you have one like Paul, it might be a good part to tell). You should describe interacting with Jesus and a moment when you were changed by him.

My conversion story is not very satisfying. It sounds like this.

Preliminary situation: I was born in California.

Initial incident: My parents told me about Jesus and that I could live forever with him in heaven.

Crisis: I knew I had done some wrong in my life, like stolen a chocolate chip cookie. I understood that if I did wrong things I would go to hell. Yikes.

Climax: I had to decide whether to pray to receive Jesus into my heart. I did.

Denouement: Then I lived for several more decades and had a family and did some things.

It's not a particularly good story, so let's try this one.

Preliminary situation: I moved away to college.

Initial incident: It had been implied to me in the "Christian bubble" that those on the outside were evil, horrible people. I discovered firsthand that they were broken and sinful (just like inside the bubble), but many were good and interesting and kind and loving. This made me question everything else I had learned from Christians as a child.

Crises: A variety of temptations arose, some related to belief and some to action. Would I continue to believe in Jesus? Would I adopt a new morality? Would I experiment with new sinful behaviors?

Climax: A youth pastor asked me to be involved in mentoring youth, an invitation he made out of love for me even though I was not qualified. I knew I needed to make a decision, because to mentor the youth well meant I had to decide whether to follow Jesus. This question forced me to struggle through a variety of issues and reengage with God.

Denouement: Through my involvement with high schoolers, I realized I wanted to go into vocational ministry and become an overseas missionary.

This isn't a conversion story, but it is a transformation story. I would flesh it out more if I were talking to a friend, but I think we can agree it's far more compelling than my conversion story.

One last warning. Don't spend a lot of time telling people your preliminary situation. It's too easy to get going on all the details that aren't part of the story. For instance, I have two sisters who were in high school when I started college. I actually went to a junior college for two years before transferring. My dad drove me down to school. That first night in the dorms he stayed in my room while I went down with all the other students to see a movie projected on a sheet. It was *The Crow.* That's how I met some of my dorm mates for the first time. I didn't have a roommate. It was a coed dorm. Et cetera, et cetera. None of that is the story. It can be good to set a few things up, but we all find our own details far more interesting than others do.

If you want to emphasize part of your story, it should be the initial incident and the climax. Like this:

Initial incident: A friend introduced me to drugs. Climax: I stood before the judge, strung out and disbelieving as he handed down my sentence. I could choose between jail and rehab.

Initial incident: I went on a summer mission trip to Haiti. Climax: I knew God was asking me to come back to work in an orphanage for a year. I had to make a decision.

Initial incident: My father died when I was young, and I hated God because of that. Climax: I sat on the side of the road in my car yelling at God, begging him to talk to me.

Initial incident: My first child was born.

Initial incident: I got a scholarship.

Initial incident: Someone broke into my house.

Initial incident: I read a book/saw a movie/went to a play that made me think about life.

Initial incident: I got hurt and couldn't play sports anymore.

Climax: God intervened and everything changed.

For many of us, our stories end with *deus ex machina*. "Then God showed up." That's OK. In fact, it's beautiful.

So what's your story about the good news? What's your story about Jesus?

15

Frayed

Theo,

There is perhaps no better story to explain to you Paul's single-minded devotion to the good news of Jesus than this: during a magnificent storm, he moved a food cart along the aisle of a storm-wracked plane.

A soldier named Captain Julius had been put in charge of taking Paul and a variety of prisoners on the journey to their day of reckoning. It was decided that the easiest and quickest way to transport so many of us (I was allowed to join the party) was to commandeer a commercial airliner.

A few hours into the flight, the ship's captain informed us it might be bumpy and to make sure our seat belts were fastened. We did. It was not just bumpy; it was terrifying. The plane dropped ten or twenty feet at a time, and Paul was not the only one praying. Out my window, I could see the wings bending in the wind.

In the midst of this, Paul stood and said, "As I prayed, an angel of God came to me and told me that I must make it to trial. God has graciously allowed that every person on this plane will survive this storm." The sound of stressed metal groaning filled the cabin. "Don't be afraid. We won't die. But this plane will crash."

Paul emerged a few minutes later with a cart full of food. It thrashed about in the aisle, and more than once Paul fell against the seats on either side. "Gentlemen," he said. "You're going to need your strength when we land this thing, so you need to eat some food." In answer, one of the men retched into an airsickness bag. Paul nodded. "I understand that you're not hungry, but you must try." Paul picked up a roll of bread from the cart and held it up. He prayed for the food, then took a bite, eating it almost like a show, reminding us how one eats.

Then he rolled the cart down the aisle, delivering food to each of us.

No sooner did we finish eating than the alarm began to sound. Oxygen masks fell from the ceiling. Paul rushed to his seat, but the plane was bouncing hard now. I saw him fly up and hit the roof, then fall again onto the armrest of a chair. The prisoner in that seat grabbed Paul by the jumpsuit, steadying him, and Paul quickly fell into the seat next to me and buckled his belt.

There was a screaming sound, followed by a massive change in the air pressure. Bits of paper and anything not screwed into the metal flew out the tear in the fuselage. I put on the mask and breathed the plastic-tinged air. I looked at Paul, panicked, and he smiled at me through his mask, clapped me on the back, and gave me a thumbs-up. "Your hair won't even get messed up," he said, then tucked himself into crash position.

It was not a pleasant landing. We hit the water hard, and the plane began to sink immediately. Captain Julius and his soldiers were on their feet within seconds, pulling prisoners to their feet, unlocking handcuffs, and moving people toward the emergency exit. The water was already knee-deep in the plane.

I grabbed the flotation device under my seat, a small square bit of safety against the gray sea outside. Paul was bent over, peering out the oval window. He turned to me, grinning. The man knew no fear once God had spoken to him. "I see land," he said. Then he announced to the passengers, "We'll all be fine, just as my God promised."

Two hundred and seventy-six of us made it to the island, the entire plane. We watched the fuselage make its final dive, disappearing in the gray, pounding rain. Captain Julius organized us into groups and did a head count to make sure all had survived and none were missing. Some of the homeowners from nearby arrived with blankets and hot drinks. The captain did not want to split us up at this point—he couldn't afford to lose any prisoners—so he asked that they bring down tents and start a fire rather than welcome us into their homes. They brought down tarps and awnings and then showed us great kindness by building a bonfire. Paul and some of the others helped.

As Paul grabbed an armful of brush to throw on the fire, a great, triangle-headed snake leapt out of the brush, fangs bared, and bit Paul's hand. I will never forget this picture. Paul, in his orange jumpsuit, backlit by the fire, standing there staring at the viper, which was hanging from his hand by its fangs. He didn't scream or shout. He merely pulled his hand back and flung it forward toward the fire. The snake pinwheeled off his hand and into the red-hot center of the coals.

I stood beside a man who lived on the island we had landed on, and he said, "That man must deserve to die, because he survived the plane crash only to be bitten by that snake. He must be a murderer to have that sort of karma."

I examined the wound. Two clear punctures, as you would expect. But not a bit of redness or swelling. Paul suffered no ill effects from the bite, and soon enough the rumor circulated among the islanders that he was a god. When Paul heard, he looked at me and sighed, his hair plastered to his head in the rain, a look of immense fatigue on his face.

Eventually, the governor of that province arrived and, taking stock of the situation, assured the captain that there was room for all of us at his estate. When we arrived, Paul heard that the governor's father was sick in bed with dysentery, so he quietly excused himself and found the father's room, prayed for him, and came back to join us. Of course, the man was healed, and in the morning, every sick person on the island stood at the governor's front door. They too were cured, and the entire time we remained on that island, Paul preached and taught the good news about Jesus. Which he continued to do the entire way to our destination.

He was allowed to have his own apartment while he waited for his case to be heard, but he was under house arrest, and had to wear a tracking bracelet day and night. So Paul hosted people in his home, telling them the good news about Jesus, occasionally stopping to rearrange the tracker on his ankle as he emphasized this or that point about the good news of freedom.

Unraveling

Gustav Freytag called the end of a story the denouement, which is a French word meaning "to come unraveled." It's the moment when every knot in the plot comes untied. The book of Acts doesn't do that particularly well as it moves toward its ending. In fact, it ends relatively suddenly. We've been told for many chapters that we're moving toward a dramatic end: Paul on trial before Caesar, the highest authority in the empire! He'll share the good news with him, and who knows what might happen?

There's a lot of excitement as we move toward the end, with riots and beatings and shipwrecks and poisonous snakes, but no trial. Caesar never appears. Paul sits in his rented home for two years, something mentioned in an almost throwaway sentence.

It's possible that this was the result of Luke deciding that it was time to get this thing finished and off to Theophilus. Every day Luke showed up at Paul's rented place, wondering if this was the day that something amazing would happen. Instead, it was the same old thing. The same old, boring, everyday thing. Paul shared the good news. People followed Jesus. The lame walked, the blind could see, the deaf could hear. The good news continued to go out, and no one could stand against it. The Holy Spirit spoke. Ordinary people did ordinary things empowered by the Holy Spirit.

The book of Acts is full of many other stories Luke told that we don't have space to cover in this book—amazing, wonderful stories of the everyday presence of the Holy Spirit. Priscilla and Aquila. The seven sons of Sceva getting beaten up by demons because they try to do an exorcism without the presence of the Holy Spirit, using the name of Jesus like a magical talisman. Riots in Ephesus. Peter released from jail by an angel so he can spread the good news. Paul remaining in prison after an earthquake so he can share the good news. Eutychus, who falls asleep in a stuffy room while listening to yet another of Paul's sermons and falls out the window, landing on the ground dead and waking up when the Holy Spirit raises him from the dead in response to Paul's prayers. Paul running out of money at one point and spending two verses as a tent maker, jumping immediately back into full-time ministry the second his friends show up with more money. Paul and Barnabas fighting over whether to give a young man named John Mark a second chance—Paul's enough of a jerk about it that they separate, and Paul and Silas on the one hand and Barnabas and John Mark on the other go on to have amazing ministries in the power of the Holy Spirit.

As Luke pens the final words of his book, opposition to the good news and the followers of Jesus is growing. Riots in the Roman Empire are on the rise. Nero, the same emperor who will release

Paul, is only a handful of years away from blaming Christians for everything wrong in the empire, leading to an unprecedented time of state-approved persecution, torture, and murder of Christians.

None of that matters. Whether nothing hinders the community of faith or they are opposed by one another, other religions, or the state, they do the same thing. Whether they have money or nothing, whether they are in jail or free, whether there are internal disputes or external threats, the people of God do the same thing over and over in every story: empowered by the Holy Spirit, they share the good news.

There is no one off-limits to them.

There is no evildoer so heinous they write them off.

There is no barrier sufficient to stop them, not even death itself.

Peter will die, and the Word of God will continue to spread.

Paul will be executed, but the Holy Spirit will continue to speak.

And the same words that are spoken in the final verse of Acts will continue to be true of all those who follow Jesus: they preached the kingdom of God boldly and taught about the Lord Jesus Christ.

They Will Listen

Every morning, Paul rises with the sun. His guard unlocks the handcuffs from the bar alongside his bed, and he showers while the guard watches, puts on his orange jumpsuit, and then is cuffed to the officer. He eats a simple breakfast, not always finishing before the first knock on his door.

The crowd of interested people seems to grow with each passing day, and they crowd into the apartment, sitting on the arms of chairs and curling up in the spaces between the furniture and the walls.

They pull out their Bibles, and Paul walks them through it. The kingdom of God, revealed by the prophets. Jesus, predicted by Moses and the law. They fight. They argue. Some believe. Some resist.

Finally, one day, Paul turns to the book of Isaiah and says, "This is the verse that reminds me of you who continue to resist. God says that your hearts have become calloused so that you hear the good news but don't understand it. You see it but don't process the sight correctly. You've stopped up your ears and closed your eyes. If that weren't the case, you might see with your eyes, hear with your ears, and understand with your hearts, and God would turn toward you and heal you.

"I want you to know," Paul says, "you think you're God's people, but you don't hear what God says. So God will send his saving words to those who don't know him, and they will listen!"

And that, my friend, is precisely what has happened, what is happening, what will continue to happen, by the power of our beloved Holy Spirit.

Postscript

Theo,

Aristotle says there are three parts to a story: the beginning, the middle, and the end. In this story, knowing where to write "The End" is a special challenge, because this is the story of the Holy Spirit. Just as he has no beginning, his story does not end. For years to come, he will continue to work, revealing things to his people, enlightening those who do not yet know him, teaching and convicting and empowering.

We never expected our greatest lesson. It was a simple realization: we cannot change the world without being changed ourselves. We are not separate from the world we are changing. We are a part of the creation. As the Holy Spirit transforms creation, we too are being transformed. Is it any surprise that we who are closest to him, who are filled with him, baptized in him, surrounded by him, empowered by him will experience the most violent, the most sudden, the most constant transformation as we move ever closer to the likeness of God?

So our prayer must be that God will allow us to share his wondrous good news with courage and without hindrance. May it be so. May he grant us boldness. And may nothing hinder us—our prejudices, our enemies, our pet theologies, our laws, our preferences, our very selves!

Acknowledgments

Krista, I know this isn't "take me to the riots," but I hope it's close! I've always appreciated your gift of faith and steady encouragement. I'm proud of your theological work and your gift of teaching. I'm excited to read the book you write! I'm thinking . . . history of women in mission?

To my daughters, Myca, Allie, and Zoey: I pray you will grow up to be strong voices for Jesus in your churches, your faith communities, and your circle of friends. Don't let anyone look down on you because of your youth. Or your gender. Go get 'em.

Mom and Dad, I would never be able to write a book without the space, love, and care you provide our family. Thank you!

JR. Forasteros and Clay Morgan, I love to hear "What is up, everybody?" each week, and it's always a thrill to hear, "Yo, dude." Thanks for listening and for your great ideas and input.

Shasta Kramer, thank you for helping me sort things out when I'm processing and for your encouraging words. You have the heart and spirit of Kapi'olani. Aloha.

Rabbi Eliyahu Fink, thank you for your patience and your friendship. I learn something new every time we talk. Thank you for treating me with respect and kindness. I am thankful for your presence in my life and for your spiritual insights.

James Korsmo, you worked hard on this one, and it shows. The book is immensely better for your feedback and your honest questions. Thank you for helping me to say what I meant and to drop the distractions. I really appreciate the whole Baker Books team. Thank you!

Thank you, Sandy Richter, Marc Cortez, and Gerry Breshears. I appreciate your taking the time to respond to my questions. All theological errors, of course, remain my own.

Thanks to all of you, my readers. Please don't hesitate to reach out to me! God bless us all, and may the Holy Spirit continue to fill us with wonder at the good news and give us boldness to share it.

Discussion Guide

Chapter 1: Beautiful Feet on Distant Mountains

1. Can you remember a time when someone delivered good news to you? What was the good news? How did you respond?
2. What is your definition of the gospel?
3. What do you think of the author's contention that every insight about Jesus is actually the good news?
4. Do you prefer to use the word *gospel* or *good news*? Why?

Chapter 2: The Origin of Fire

1. Read Acts 1. What do you think of the idea that the book of Acts is, first and foremost, a story about the Holy Spirit? Does that change anything as you read this passage?
2. How do you think you would have felt at the moment of Pentecost, when everyone in the church started preaching, men and women, together, in different languages on the street?

Excited? Scared? Nervous? What would it look like at your church (or home group, or wherever you worship) if everyone in the community preached?

3. What do you think of the idea that the good news is primarily the story about Jesus rather than a list of theological beliefs? Would that change the way you talk with a nonbeliever about Jesus?

4. Practice telling the story of Jesus with others in your group.

Chapter 3: Ordinary Earthquakes

1. Read Acts 3–4:31. Have you ever been healed or known someone who was? Tell us about that. Do you not believe that such things happen today? Tell us about that.

2. The author writes that he loves the idea of having his sins "wiped out" rather than forgiven. How about you? Which do you like better? Why?

3. Do you see it as blessing or condemnation when Jesus "turns you from your wicked ways"? Do you find yourself happier or miserable when you turn your sins over to God? Do you have an example you'd be willing to share?

4. According to Acts 4:13, Peter and John were seen as "unschooled, ordinary" people. How about you? Are you ordinary? What does this story teach about ordinary people who are in close proximity to Jesus?

Chapter 4: Dead Money

1. Read Acts 4:32–5:11. How do you feel about this story? What questions do you have as you read it?

2. What do you think of the proposal that the sin of Ananias and Sapphira was not only that they lied but also that they lied to gain status in the community of faith? Do you agree or disagree? Why?

3. Do you have places in your life that you hide from people in church? Why? Who do you feel comfortable sharing your whole self with?

4. Do you see the sin of Ananias and Sapphira in your own church? In the community of faith nationwide? Worldwide?

Chapter 5: The Outlaws

1. Read Acts 5:12–42. What stands out to you about this story?

2. What are the potential consequences of sharing the good news of Jesus illegally in "closed countries"? Do you think it's worth the cost?

3. What do you make of the story of Samuel being told by God to emphasize sacrificing a heifer over anointing King David? Does that make sense to you? Make you uncomfortable?

4. What do you think of the author's assertion that we can break the law without being dishonest? Do you agree or disagree? Why?

Chapter 6: Waiters and Parking Lot Attendants

1. Read Acts 6–7. What would you do if your church multiplied by twenty-five overnight? What problems would you expect? How would you deal with the influx of people?

2. Brainstorm who in your community is in the minority (not just by ethnicity but by social class, marital status, age, etc.).

What needs might they have that the majority is overlooking? Are you willing to form a relationship with them and ask them what their needs are? How can your community empower them to make sure their needs are taken care of?

3. Do you buy the author's argument that we should not be gospel- or Bible-centered but rather centered on Jesus? How might this shift the way we speak about things? How we do things?

4. Do you believe that ordinary people, empowered by the Spirit, can change the world? How?

Chapter 7: The Effeminate Foreigner

1. Read Acts 8:26–40. It's hard to read this passage without thinking about people of various sexual preferences. Do you think this passage speaks to that at all? Why or why not?

2. How does Philip's interaction with the eunuch differ from the way the eunuch was received in Jerusalem? What do you think that felt like for the eunuch?

3. Do you think it would have made much difference in this story if Philip had been "Bible-centered" instead of Christ-centered?

4. What outsiders can you think of in your own culture who may not know they are able to approach God? How could you best convince them otherwise?

Chapter 8: Those Who Are Far Off

1. Read Acts 9:1–19. List all the people you can think of who would fall into the category "enemies of God."

2. Given this story, how do you think God might choose to deal with his enemies?

3. What if God asked you to pray for healing for one of his enemies? How would you respond? Who would be hardest for you to approach if God were to ask that of you?

4. How can you best take the good news about Jesus to the enemies of God?

Chapter 9: The Sail

1. Read Acts 9:32–10:48. The author says that one of the lessons of this passage is that there is no such thing as an "unclean" person. Do you think that's a good interpretation? Why or why not?

2. Who are the people in your life, community, or church who are treated as if they are lesser than others? What should be done about that?

3. What do you think of Peter's description of the good news as "Jesus is Lord of all" (Acts 10:36)?

4. Are there people in the world who you would be surprised if God gave them the gift of the Holy Spirit? Who? Why?

Chapter 10: Hero Worship

1. Read Acts 14:8–20. Have you ever known someone who was so Christlike that it seemed like they were from another world? What was that experience like?

2. How do you feel when people you respect in spiritual roles reveal their own weaknesses and sins? Share an example when this happened. Remember, of course, that you are sharing

your story, not theirs, and please be mindful of other people's privacy.

3. Have you had to deal with moments of hero worship when others looked up to you in an unhealthy way? How did you deal with this?

4. Does your faith community have a healthy perspective on those in spiritual authority? Do they respect them without worshiping them? Do they recognize they are human beings and not demigods?

Chapter 11: Breaking the Law

1. Read Acts 15. Do you feel nervous when we talk about "the rules"? Does it make you feel strange that the author says the Twelve didn't think non-Jews needed to follow the Ten Commandments?

2. The author says legalism can be good, especially for teaching people like children boundaries. Can you think of other times legalistic rules might be helpful? Is there a time when those rules stop being of use?

3. The author shares a metaphor in which sin is a cliff and well-meaning protections (fences) are put up to protect us. He says that crossing the fences is not inherently sinful, and it's legalism to say that it is. Take a few obvious sins (do not murder, do not steal, do not commit sexual immorality, do not worship idols) and talk about what fences might look like for those sins. Do you agree that crossing those fences is not sinful?

4. For most of us, legalism is part of growing up (we all used to hold someone's hand when crossing the street). Share a story of legalism in your own past (or present). How did you move beyond it?

Chapter 12: Stealing Zeus

1. Read Acts 17. How did you feel in the story portion at the beginning of this chapter when Paul quoted from the Hindu Vedas? Excited? Nervous? Confused?

2. The author says that we shouldn't be afraid to study other religions and that it shows people respect when we expect them to hear the good news about God. Do you agree or disagree? Why?

3. The author says there is truth in all religions and that truth leads to Christ. What do you think? How do you come to that conclusion?

4. Acts 17:26–27 says that God has chosen the times and places when and where all people live so that they will seek and maybe find him. Tell us that story about your own life. How did the time and place of your birth and upbringing allow you to come to Jesus?

Chapter 13: Upside Down

1. Read Acts 25–26.

2. Paul was told that he had been chosen to be a witness of his experience with Jesus. How would you tell the good news to someone using your own story?

3. "Turn to God and show it by your actions." Do you think this sentence has the potential to change the world? How? Do you think it would turn things upside down in your family? At work? In politics? In the world?

4. What would it look like to tell people the good news without embarrassment, with boldness, and with simplicity? Give an example.

Chapter 14: The Story Tellers

1. For this week's discussion, use the story structure to create your own story that reveals the good news of Jesus. What is your preliminary situation (what we need to know before the story starts)?
2. Initial incident (what starts the story)?
3. Crises (problems along the way)?
4. Climax (the biggest problem you faced)?
5. Denouement (the world since then)?

Chapter 15: Frayed

1. The author describes Paul's imprisonment as two years of the "same old thing"—people coming to Christ, miracles, the good news going out. Is it possible we've lost sight of the wonder of the amazing things God is doing among us? Share three stories of amazing things God has done in the last two years.
2. What stories in Acts don't appear in this book that you wish had been included? How would you retell those stories? What lessons do you learn from them?
3. How can you be part of sharing the good news with boldness?
4. What insights are you taking away from this book and our time discussing it?

Notes

Chapter 1 Beautiful Feet on Distant Mountains

1. It's possible, depending on the translation of your Bible, that it might say something other than "good news" or "gospel" here. It might just say "proclaiming." But I assure you that the word in Greek is *euangelizomenoi*, which means "proclaiming the good news."

Chapter 2 The Origin of Fire

1. In fact, outside his own writings, Paul is referred to as an apostle only twice, both times in the book of Acts (14:4, 14). In these instances, Luke appears to be using the word in its literal meaning, "one who has been sent," and not in the sense that it is used elsewhere in Acts when "the apostles" refers to the Twelve and their role as leaders in the community of God. Which is not to say that Luke didn't think of Paul as an apostle (obviously he did); but it does go to show the larger point that if someone said "I'm going to write a book about the apostles," people at the time would have likely thought, "Oh, a book about the Twelve. That should be interesting." It's unlikely Luke would have titled his letter "Acts of the Apostles."

Chapter 7 The Effeminate Foreigner

1. Acts 8:32–33, quoting Isa. 53:7–8.
2. Isa. 53:2–3.

3. For a really interesting article on the Nubian warrior queens, see Carolyn Fluehr-Lobban, "Nubian Queens in the Nile Valley and Afro-Asiatic Cultural History," Ninth International Conference for Nubian Studies, August 20–26, 1998.
4. See *The Illustrated Bible Story by Story* (New York City: DK Publishing, 2012), 427.
5. *The Apostolic Tradition of Hippolytus of Rome* 21.3–5.
6. See Joseph Bingham, *Antiquities of the Christian Church* (London: Henry G. Bohn, 1846), 536.

Chapter 9 The Sail

1. Clinton E. Arnold, *Acts* (Grand Rapids: Zondervan, 2002), 90. See also Jonathan Roth, "The Size and Organization of the Roman Imperial Legion," *Historia: Zeitschrift für Alte Geschichte* 43, no. 3 (1994): 346–62.

Chapter 10 Hero Worship

1. You can find a retelling of this story in book 8 of Ovid's *Metamorphoses*, vv. 611–724.
2. Even here, I find myself pushing against that and saying, "I should mention that his university looked into it and largely exonerated him, making it clear it was more along the lines of a failure to properly annotate." Why is that? Because I have huge respect for Dr. King. I want him to be perfect instead of human.
3. I've since learned, incidentally, that "armor bearer" is a traditional office in many African American churches, especially in the South. In another context, this person might be called a "speaker's liaison." The armor bearer takes care of the pastor's needs when he's getting ready to speak. He gets the pastor water, makes sure he's got his notes, maybe picks him up at his house in the morning. It doesn't always mean that he prevents people from getting to the pastor, but if he feels it's a distraction to him getting ready to preach, he certainly will.
4. Flavius Josephus, *Antiquities* 19.343–50.
5. From Martin Luther King Jr.'s last sermon, "The Drum Major Instinct," available online at http://mlk-kpp01.stanford.edu/index.php/kingpapers/article/the_drum_major_instinct/.

Chapter 11 Breaking the Law

1. This is a common moral rule I hear. I'm baffled why "single woman" is part of the formula rather than "woman." People can't cheat on their spouse with another married person? It happens all the time. For that

matter, people cheat on their spouses with people of the same gender too. Are we not allowed to ever ride together in cars?

Chapter 12 Stealing Zeus

1. John Baxter, *Mythmaker: The Life and Work of George Lucas* (New York: Avon Books, 1999), 163–66.

2. Aratus, *Phaenomena* 1–5, in R. Faber, "The Apostle and the Poet: Paul and Aratus," *Clarion* 42, no. 13 (1993), http://spindleworks.com/library/rfaber/aratus.htm.

3. It really does! Check out Sura 19 of the Qur'an.

Chapter 13 Upside Down

1. For example, check out the article "Jesus Tradition in Paul" by David B. Capes: http://paulinetheology.blogspot.com/2007/07/jesus-and-paul.html.

THE FIRST TIME WE SAW HIM

awakening to the wonder of Jesus

gospel stories retold for today

MATT MIKALATOS

"Matt Mikalatos extracts the best-known stories of the Gospels from their ancient setting and inserts them boldly into a modern context. This is a must-read for those seeking a fresh look at the living, breathing Christ."

—**Josh D. McDowell**, author and speaker

BakerBooks
a division of Baker Publishing Group
www.BakerBooks.com

For more information
about **MATT** visit
MIKALATOS.COM